Frederick B Cowl

Digging Ditches

and other sermons to boys and girls

Frederick B Cowl

Digging Ditches
and other sermons to boys and girls

ISBN/EAN: 9783337264604

Printed in Europe, USA, Canada, Australia, Japan

Cover: Foto ©Lupo / pixelio.de

More available books at **www.hansebooks.com**

DIGGING DITCHES

DIGGING DITCHES

AND

Other Sermons to Boys and Girls

BY

REV. FREDERICK B. COWL

NEW YORK: EATON & MAINS
CINCINNATI: CURTS & JENNINGS

TO

THE BOYS AND GIRLS

OF

Holly Park Wesleyan Church

CROUCH HILL, LONDON

WHOSE ATTENTIVE HEARING HAS MANY TIMES

ENCOURAGED THE PREACHER

TO PREACH AGAIN

PREFACE

Eleven years ago, when I was associated with the Woodhouse Moor Wesleyan Church, Leeds, the Sunday school workers requested that something should be done by the minister for the children in the Sunday morning service. In response to that request, I undertook a separate sermon for the children. This I have continued to the present time, with a growing sense of the necessity for something to be done, but not always sure what it was best to do. The sermons in this volume are some of the fruit of that work. They were spoken not always to the younger children, and never to the older ones, with no pretence to literary style, but with a supreme consideration for the actual life of the boys and girls to whom they were addressed, than whom I have never found more attentive and responsive hearers.

July 1896.

CONTENTS

	PAGE
Digging Ditches	13
"Make this valley full of ditches."	
2 KINGS iii. 16.	
Full Ditches	18
"That valley shall be filled with water."	
2 KINGS iii. 17.	
Doing Our Best	23
"She hath done what she could."	
MARK xiv. 8.	
Purse-Making	27
"Make for yourselves purses which wax not old."	
LUKE xii. 33 (R.V.).	
Clay-Modelling	34
"He made it again another vessel."	
JER. xviii. 4.	
Hedge-Breakers	39
"Whoso breaketh an hedge, a serpent shall bite him."	
ECCLES. x. 8.	
Wood-Gatherers	44
"The children gather wood."	
JER. vii. 8.	

CONTENTS

	PAGE
A Chance Arrow	49

"And a certain man drew his bow at a venture, and smote the King of Israel between the joints of the harness."   1 KINGS xxii. 34.

Little by Little 54

"He that is faithful in a very little is faithful also in much."   LUKE xvi. 10 (R.V.).

Mimics 59

"Imitate not that which is evil, but that which is good."   3 John 11 (R.V.).

A Good Copy 64

"Be ye imitators of me, even as I also am of Christ."   1 COR. xi. 1 (R.V.).

The Door 69

"Jesus said . . . I am the door of the sheep."   JOHN x. 7.

Sides 74

"The Lord is on my side; I will not fear."   Ps. cxviii. 6.

Secrets 79

"The secret of the Lord is with them that fear Him."   Ps. xxv. 14.

Not Mine—Whose? 84

"Ye are not your own; for ye were bought with a price."   1 COR. vi. 19, 20.

Alas! Borrowed 89

"Alas, master! for it was borrowed."   2 KINGS vi. 5.

Sparrows 94

MATT. x. 29 and LUKE xii. 6.

Old Shoes and Clouted 100

"And old shoes and clouted upon their feet."   JOSHUA ix. 5.

CONTENTS

Lost Shields 107
"And he took away all the shields of gold which Solomon had made."   1 KINGS xiv. 26.

Apples of Gold 113
"A word fitly spoken is like apples of gold in baskets of silver."   PROV. xxv. 11 (R.V.).

Second 118
"I shall be next unto thee."   1 SAM. xxiii. 17.

A Riddle 124
"Out of the eater came forth meat, and out of the strong came forth sweetness."   JUDGES xiv. 14.

Clean Hands 130
"He that hath clean hands shall be stronger and stronger."   JOB xvii. 9.

A Pure Heart 135
"He that hath clean hands, and a pure heart."   Ps. xxiv. 4.

Copper Precious as Gold 140
"Two vessels of fine bright brass, precious as gold."   EZRA viii. 27 (R.V.).

Straight Away 146
"And straightway they left the nets and followed Him."   MARK i. 18.

Dog 151
"Beware of the dogs."   PHIL. iii. 2 (R.V.).

Remember 155
"Remember Jesus Christ."   2 TIM. ii. 8 (R.V.).

Digging Ditches

"Make this valley full of ditches."
2 Kings iii. 16.

There is a stirring soldier story in connection with this verse which I will, in a few words, tell you.

Mesha, king of Moab, had to pay a large tribute of wool to the king of Israel. After the death of Ahab, he rebelled and withheld the tribute. Then Jehoram, king of Israel, persuaded the kings of Judah and Edom to go with him against Mesha. After a march of seven days, they came to the valley which divided Edom from Moab. They depended upon finding water in this valley, and brought, therefore, no supply with them; but when the soldiers got to their camping-ground, weary and thirsty, they found the stream dried up. Too exhausted to retreat, and too thirsty to fight, with their enemies in view on the opposite hills, Jehoram foolishly and complainingly said, "Alas, that the Lord hath called these three kings together, to deliver them into the hand of Moab."

But the king of Judah was a better man, and asked whether there was not a prophet of the Lord, so that they might inquire of the Lord through him. Sturdy

Elisha was there, and to him the three kings went. He reproved Jehoram for coming, because he was wicked, and did not think of God when things were prosperous.

Is it not mean, boys and girls, to come to God only when we are in trouble, and forget Him at other times? Let none of us do this.

However, for the sake of Jehoshaphat, the good man of the three (good people are worth having in our company), Elisha asked the Lord what they were to do. The answer God gave him was, that they were to make the valley full of ditches; because, though there would be no sign or sound of rain, yet the valley would be full of water, and they should drink themselves, and their cattle, and their beasts. And then the Lord would deliver their enemies into their hand.

Now, the picture I want you to see and remember is that of these thirsty soldiers digging ditches in this dry valley; and as you look at them, remember—

First. What we are to be.

We must all be diggers. Everything worth having has to be worked for. Getting knowledge is like digging; for lessons, as boys and girls well know, have to be learned. There are a few clever boys in every school, who seem as if lessons come naturally to them, and the first place in the class is as easy to them as the last place to another. But these are exceptions. The surest way to the top is by hard work—getting our spade in and digging like thirsty soldiers. The duffer is the boy without spade. The prize-winner is the boy with spade, who has dug hard.

Becoming good is like digging. When we pray, read our Bibles, try to do right, we are diggers. If we are lazy about goodness, we shall no more become good than we shall become wise if we don't learn lessons.

Once during the American revolution a little squad of soldiers were trying to lift a heavy beam to its place. The officer in charge was giving loud orders. A gentleman in private dress came by and asked the officer why he didn't help. "Sir," said he, " I am a corporal." The gentleman took off his coat, helped the soldiers, and then, turning to the corporal, said, "When you have another such job, send for the Commander-in-Chief, and he will come and help you again."

Orders, of course, must be given, but we must not be above work—whoever we are, let us be amongst the diggers.

By learning and reading and thinking, by prayer and Bible and sermon, let us make the valley of our life full of trenches for the rain to fill.

Secondly, some ditches which we must dig.

(*a*) The lesson ditch.

Old men say to us, " Learn, learn all you can while young." So say I, though not old yet. Learn not merely from school-books, but from other books, and not merely from books, but from people and from nature also; for birds and flowers, sky and sea, mountain and valley, have many lessons to teach,

Make, then, as many ditches as time will let you. When I was a small boy at school, Latin seemed very dry and hard, so I asked the headmaster to let me give it up, as I should not need it. He said, "No, keep on with it; you don't know what use it may be." The first thing I wanted after school-days was my bit of Latin that I had worked hard at until I liked it, and so the Latin ditch was not in vain.

(*b*) Obedience is a ditch we must dig. It is tiresome not to be allowed to do as we like, but it is best. Let us learn to obey, though we can't always see the use of it. We shall be thirsty soldiers all our life unless we have dug a deep, deep ditch of obedience.

As some boys were playing marbles, the rain came on. Fred, one of the youngest, said, "I must go home; mother said I must not go out in the rain." "Your mother—fudge! the rain won't hurt you any more than it will us," shouted the others. "I'll not disobey my mother for any of you," was the quick reply.

That is the kind of ditch to dig. God will fill it by and by with His own rain.

(*c*) Faith is another ditch for our valley. Let us learn to think about God and to believe in Him; read what He says about Himself in the Bible; and find out what He is like in the life of Jesus, until our hearts can trust in Him.

This is the most important ditch of all, and we shall need it more than any other by and by.

There are many Bible trenches we may dig to feed

this faith-ditch. When we learn Ps. xxiii., Isa. liii., John xiv. and xv., 1 Cor. xiii., we are digging precious ditches.

A very little friend of mine has begun her digging early, for she is not three years old. When her nurse asked her the other day whom she loved, her reply was, " I love Jesus; do oo, Nana ? "

We cannot dig ditches of love and trust too soon or too deep.

Let us all make our " Valley full of ditches," and by and by we shall find them filled with rain.

Full Ditches

"That valley shall be filled with water."
2 KINGS iii. 17.

THERE were no clouds telling of rain, no wind that had the sound of rain in it, and the valley was very dry. How tired those soldiers must have got of their ditch-digging! And most likely some of them became cross as well. But God had said, "Make the valley full of ditches," because though they should "not see wind neither see rain, yet that valley should be filled with water."

And so it was. During the night, as the tired diggers slept, rain fell up among the hills, and came rushing in a mountain torrent down the valley, filling up all their trenches, and then away it went.

So it will be, boys and girls, in reference to the ditches of which we were speaking in our last sermon. They shall be filled.

1. Our *Home ditches* will fill.

The best and happiest men have had to thank God for the ditches they had to dig at home.

When they have gone out into the world, and have had to obey masters, to be at work punctually, and to do things with exact care, they have said, "Thank God, my mother made me obey, taught me to be thorough, and to keep time."

"There," said Harry, throwing down the shoe-brush "that'll do. My shoes don't look very bright, but no matter. Who cares?"

"My boy," said his father, who had overheard what he said to himself, "your shoes look wretchedly. Pick up the brush, and make them shine. When you have finished, come into the house."

He made them shine, and went to his father, who said, "I have a little story to tell you. I once knew a poor boy, whose mother taught him that whatever is worth doing is worth doing well. This boy went out to service in a gentleman's family, and he took pains to do everything well, no matter how unimportant it seemed. His employer was pleased, and took him into his shop. So he advanced from step to step, until he became a clerk, and then a partner in the business. He is now a rich man, and anxious that his son Harry should learn to practise the rule which made him prosper."

"Why, father, were you a poor boy once?"

"Yes, my son, so poor that I had to go out to service, and black boots, and wait at table, and do any menial service that was required of me. By doing little things well, I was soon trusted with more important ones."

So the ditch he dug at home, which at the time seemed no use, was filled with prosperity.

2. *School ditches* will fill also.

Lessons are often hard, but some of the hardest, if we work hard at them, will become very enjoyable. And then knowledge will be like God's rain filling the lesson ditch.

To know, and be able to do because we know, will be to have a *very* full ditch.

Who would care to be a dunce? Who would like to stand on the form wearing a tall cap because he didn't know anything? But the dunce is the boy who has not dug any ditches. If we dig them, knowledge will fill them. Don't mind, then, the hard school-digging, for the reward will come.

3. *Bible ditches* will fill.

In later life, when duties are many, sorrows heavy, and temptations severe, the promises and precepts we have stored away in childhood will come back to help and cheer us.

We are inclined to say now, "What's the use of so much praying and reading?" Dig away, and some day you will say, "God has filled my ditch."

Kindness, too, is a trench which will be filled some day.

I will tell you a story of a ditch well filled. Many years ago, a lady, sitting in the coach which ran between Glasgow and Greenock, noticed, when just past Bishopton, a barefooted, tired boy struggling along the road. She paid for a seat for him on the coach. At Greenock she asked him what he was going to do. He said he wished to be a sailor. She gave him half a crown, and wished him well. Twenty years afterwards the coach was going to Glasgow, and near Bishopton one of the passengers, a sea captain, saw an old lady wearily walking along the road. He paid for a seat for her. While the horses were changed at Bishopton, the captain talked to her, and she thanked him for his kindness. He told her how, twenty years ago, a lady gave him a seat and paid for it. "Well do I remember that," said she. "I am that lady, reduced to poverty by the doings of a prodigal son." "I," said the captain, "have been successful, and am retiring home to live on my fortune; and from this day I shall bind myself and heirs to supply you with twenty-five pounds per annum till your death."

Thus the old lady's ditch of kindness was—after twenty years—filled.

God will reward all our true and earnest digging; and the promise of that reward should cheer us to dig.

These soldiers were helped in their hard digging by this promise of rain. So all workers are cheered by the promise of reward. The farmer ploughs and sows, because God has promised that harvest shall not cease. I have seen children by the sea digging deep, long ditches with ever so much care, though there was no water in them. But they knew the tide would soon be coming in. And what joy when the first wave reached their first trench!

When you are busy at home or in school, in work for yourself or others, remember the promise, "The valley shall be filled with water."

Doing Our Best

"She hath done what she could."
MARK xiv. 8.

MARY, the sister of Lazarus, had just simply brought an alabaster cruse of precious ointment, and after Eastern fashion, poured it over Christ's head. In this way she showed her love to Him. Some of the people thought it foolish and wasteful. The cruse was worth about ten pounds, and could have been sold and the money given to the poor.

But Christ would not have her blamed, and said that throughout the world her act should be spoken of. Why? Christ could have done without the anointing very well. He had not counted how much it was worth. He loved the deed, because she had done her best.

This answers two important questions in the life of each one of us—namely, How can we get on? and how can we win the approval of those about us?

1. There are many things we cannot do we should like to do, but we can do our best.

"If I could paint like a Doré, I would paint," says one. "If I could play cricket like Grace, I should be a cricketer," says another. "If I could learn like the cleverest in the class, I should work hard," says a third.

And so we don't paint or cricket or work, because we can't be of the first ones. But that is not the way at all. The great thing is that we should do our best, and we shall be sure to accomplish something worth while.

When Mr. Gladstone was giving the prizes at a Wimbledon school, he asked the boys this question, "If you were told to jump, what would you do?" The eager reply of the boys was, "We would jump as high as ever we could."

Yes, that's it. Not as high as Smith the champion, but "as high as ever we could." That is doing their best. It is only when we do things lazily and slovenly that we need be ashamed of them. .

There was a member of the House of Commons who had risen from very lowly life by his diligence and perseverance, and made for himself an honourable name. He was taunted one day by a man of higher birth, who ought to have had better manners, with his humble origin. "I remember," said he, "when you blacked my father's boots." "Well, sir," was the gentlemanly reply, "*did I not do it well?*"

He was not ashamed of his boot-cleaning, since he knew he did his best at it.

Boys and girls, always remember that the lowliest service is high and honourable, if we bring a true spirit to it and do our level best.

2. Another thing Christ's defence of Mary proves; that it was not the deed itself that made it approved, but because it was the best she could do.

If the cruse had been worth much less, and yet her best, Christ would have loved it equally. You remember His praise of the poor woman who gave only two mites. But they were her best, and Christ therefore approved them more than the greater gifts.

If we do a great thing which is not our best, it is small. Someone looking over the map you have drawn at school says, "It is very good," but the master, standing by, says, "No; it would have been good for a lower boy in the class, but he could have done better."

If, on the other hand, your best is small, it is really great. I have a bird worked in wool by a tiny girl. If you saw it, you might say it was poor work. But, knowing the worker, I say, " No, it is very, very good."

In the Flower Service the children brought wonderful flowers, — flowers arranged in baskets and in bunches charmingly; and presently a poor little unkempt child brings a very few wild flowers, unarranged and untied. The child is as great a contrast to the other children as are her flowers to theirs. But as I see her coming, I understand her need, and feel sure that the dear Christ is saying, "She hath done what she could," and that He loves her tiny gift, because it is her best.

A prince went into his vineyard to examine it. He came to the peach tree and said, "What are you doing for me?" The tree said, "In the spring I give my blossoms and fill the air with fragrance, and on my boughs hang the fruit which men will gather and carry into the palace for you." "Well done!" said the prince. To the chestnut he said, "What are you doing?" "I am making nests for the birds, and shelter cattle with my leaves and spreading branches." "Well done!" said the prince. Then he went down to the meadow, and asked the grass what it was doing' "We are giving up our lives for others, for your sheep and cattle, that they may be nourished"; and the prince said, "Well done!" Last of all, he asked the tiny daisy what it was doing, and the daisy said, "Nothing, nothing. I cannot make a nesting-place for the birds, and I cannot give shelter to the cattle, and I cannot send fruit into the palace, and I cannot even give food for the sheep and the cows—they do not want me in the meadow. All I can do is to be the best little daisy I can be." And the prince bent down and kissed the daisy, and said, "*There is none better than thou.*"

Do not let us be discouraged if we cannot do what some others do, or if we have not what others have. Be, and do your best.

> "That man is blest
> Who does his best,
> And leaves the rest,
> And doesn't worry."

Purse-Making

"Make for yourselves purses which wax not old."
LUKE xii. 33 (R.V.).

SOMETHING we are to make both by ourselves, and for ourselves. What boy or girl is there who has not had the joy of making something all by themselves?

Do you not remember the joy you felt when you finished your first piece of woolwork all by yourself?

I have seen more boys than one with knife, hammer, and saw, boat-building on their own account. And when out of a rough piece of wood there came a somewhat shapeful boat, what joy the builder felt! He looks at it with pride and says, "Not so bad." The keel is not quite even nor the mast quite straight, and on the water she lists a little, but none of these imperfections mar much the joy of having made something, nor the pride with which he shows it to his sister, saying, "I made it all myself, and no one helped me."

And then something *for* ourselves. Not selfishly or greedily, but something we need. Girls understand better than boys the joy of having made, for instance, the first garment for themselves, which saves toil and expense to someone else.

So Christ's beautiful saying reminds us of these two things, Made by myself and for myself.

Let me ask you to think about two things. *First*, What we are to make; and *secondly*, Why we are to make it.

First, What we are to make.

"Make for yourselves *purses*." I don't think I ever knew anyone fond of making purses. I have known them make marble-bags and book-bags, but never a purse. Whether it is that purses are so cheap, it is not worth the trouble to make our own; or that money is so scarce we do not like to risk it in a self-made purse, I don't know. But there is the fact that few people make their own purses.

Christ wants us to be busy purse-making. The kind of purse Christ means is suggested to us in the following words—"that wax not old." I asked a little maiden if she knew the meaning of "wax" and her quick, sprightly reply was, "Oh yes; my doll is made of wax." But that is not quite the meaning here. We should say, in our modern English, "purses that grow not old."

Then we may be quite sure Christ does not mean

ordinary purses. Did any of my young friends ever know a purse that would keep always new? No; we can get purses of various material—leather or paper, silk or wool, cotton or velvet, ivory or tortoiseshell, purses of all sizes and shapes, and they are all alike in this, that they grow old. They become dirty and faded, holey and insecure, so that by and by you throw them aside for others, newer and better.

But the purses Christ speaks of never get old. What are they? Where can we get material from to make them?

Look at Christ's verse and you have the answer. "Sell that ye have and give alms," says Christ. As if all they gave away to others would be like making ever-new purses.

It means more than that, but it is enough at present for boys and girls to remember that by doing good to others, by cheering and helping those about us, we are "making purses which wax not old." Every kind word, each unselfish deed is like such a purse. Instead of spending all your money on yourself at Christmas, you sent a doll to the poor cripple child in the city; instead of taking your innings at cricket, you gave it up to another who had been unlucky in not getting a game; instead of going out to play, you stayed in and read to your sick mother; instead of spending the sixpence given you on some white mice which you much wished to have, you gave it to the poor children's country holiday fund. All these are purses which never grow old.

Secondly, Why make these purses?

What do you make any purses for? To carry money when you can get it. An empty purse is not much use,—indeed, it is one of the most useless things I know of. Too small for marbles and tops, for needles and cotton, for sweets and cake, it is made so thoroughly for money, and money only, that you don't seem able to make any other use of it.

The purses Christ wants us to make "for ourselves" are to carry money too—gold, silver, and copper.

The kind deed for another is the purse, remember. Now, when we have done it, it brings us pleasure. There are few joys in life like that of giving joy. The boy who heartily gives up his innings for another, enjoys it more than if he went in himself. This is the *copper* in our purse.

But our kind deed gave joy and pleasure to the one for whom it was done. How the cripple child clapped her hands over the doll you sent! The knowledge of that is the *silver* in our purse.

But Christ said, "Inasmuch as ye did it unto one of these least, ye did it unto Me." And so He approves our deed of kindness. The knowledge of that is the *gold* in our purse.

A kind deed well done will never be like an empty

purse; there will be in it more gold than silver, more silver than copper. And that is the way we like our purses to be filled.

A university student was walking one day with his professor, when they saw by a gate a coat and a pair of old shoes. The owner, a poor man, was working in the field close by.

"Let us hide his shoes," said the student, "and hide ourselves behind these bushes, and watch to see his perplexity when he cannot find them."

"My dear friend," said the professor, "we must never amuse ourselves at the expense of the poor. But you are rich, and may give yourself a much greater pleasure. Put a crown piece, if you have them, in each shoe, and *then* we will hide ourselves."

He did so, and they watched behind the bush. Presently out the man came. He put on his coat, threw off one field boot and thrust his foot into a shoe. Something hard hurt his toe. Thinking, I doubt not, some wilful boy had put in a stone, he turned up the shoe and shook out *a crown piece*. He picked it up, looked at it again and again, then about on all sides to see who had done it, but could see no one, while all the time four earnest eyes were staring at him from behind the bush. When the second shoe produced another crown piece, his astonishment was very great, and his feelings quite overcame him. "Who can have done this?" So, because he could see no one, he knelt down in the grass and he thanked God, telling Him about his sick wife and needy children, and how poor he was. I have never seen the words of his prayer, but I can imagine what it would be like.

A great, great joy came into the student's heart, and tears ran down his face; while the professor said to him, "Now, are you not better pleased than if you had played your intended trick?"

"You have taught me a lesson that I shall never forget. I feel now the truth of the words which I never before understood—'It is more blessed to give than to receive.'"

That was a purse rich in the three coins.

The great difficulty about purses is not that they become old, but that they are so empty. It is so difficult to get money to put into them.

Let your purse be as full as you can. The kind deed not merely done, but *well* done. We do some things so poorly that they are almost— if not quite — empty purses: they neither bring nor give much pleasure, nor do they win God's approval.

Speaking about these purses, once, in one of our beautiful cities, a bright little maid of about seven was in the congregation. Her auntie was to be married during the week, and she was going to give her a new white dress. When at home, the little one said, "Auntie, I shan't give you a white dress. I shall give you a lovely new purse instead, full of new gold."

May many "lovely new purses" full of new money —copper and silver and gold—be yours, boys and girls. Amen.

Clay-Modelling.

"He made it again another vessel."
JER. xviii. 4.

THERE is a very pretty picture in this text. The prophet was told by God to go down from the temple into the valley, where the potters were at work, and, while he watched the potter, God would speak to him. So he went down to the potter's house, and there he was at work. He had a large wheel fixed on an upright post, with a wooden disc in the middle, on which he placed his clay. Then the wheel was made to revolve either by hand, or by means of a treadle, and while it was spinning round, the potter, with his deft fingers and hands, moulded the clay as he wished. The prophet noticed that sometimes the vessel the potter was moulding was marred. There was a flaw in the clay, or perhaps he had not taken quite enough, or maybe a little false pressure had spoiled the vessel. Then the potter crushed the clay again into a shapeless mass, and, beginning afresh, fashioned it into another vessel, in some cases a different one altogether from that he had first intended.

We can all understand this very well. We have

many of us seen a potter at work, and if not, we have all tried our hands at clay modelling for ourselves, and know its difficulty. We have tried to make an elephant or a cow, a dog or a man. And how often after much work, we have had to double up our clay and begin again.

Hence we can all see this text: "When the vessel that he made of the clay was marred in the hand of the potter, he made it again another vessel."

Leaving the lesson which God had to teach Jeremiah from this scene in the potter's house, we may learn three things.

1. We are all like clay-modellers. Our life, with its heart and mind and soul, is the clay which we are to model into good character. We may say that the character which we have to make is the beautiful and precious vase which we model for God.

You would never think, when you see the lump of clay on the wheel disc, that the potter could make anything elegant out of it. But we know that if he is skilful he can. So can we out of our life. But we shall have to mould it. We don't become good by chance. "You cannot dream yourself into a character. You must hammer and forge yourself one."

Yes, if we are to be pure, just, loving, honourable, God-fearing, we shall have to take pains and pray about it.

We know that lessons won't be known without

learning, and we may be sure goodness won't be ours without trying.

The word "character" is from the Greek. It is used by them to express the impress made on a coin or seal by the die or mould. The head of the Queen on your penny is the "character." So in the old meaning of the word, our character is the impress we leave on ourselves by good or bad modelling.

2. We model after a pattern. The potter has either a vase before him or a pattern in his eye by which he does his present work.

"Have you," said a boy to me, "a picture of an elephant?" "What do you want it for?" "I want to mould one." Very good, for the boy who thinks he knows what an elephant is like, because he has seen one a few times, will find how little he knows when he comes to model one in real clay.

In our character-modelling we need a pattern. We have it in our knowledge of goodness. All that we know to be beautiful and right may serve us as pattern to work by.

But our knowledge may be imperfect, so we need another and better pattern as well. *Jesus Christ is our true Model.* We have to try and make our life as much like His as we can.

And while we are trying to do this, we must not forget that He is helping and working with us, and that if we give ourselves to Him, what we cannot do He will. And thus working together with us, there will be left on our life the glorious impress of Christ.

3. Our vessel may be marred. The best worker has sometimes to begin again. When we have been clay-modelling and finished our elephant, you could scarcely tell what it was; trunk and tail were so much alike, you could not tell which end was head or tail. You felt disappointed, but you began again.

It is so in character-modelling. We do not take enough clay—not enough time and care and love—to finish our vessel. We are at times *bad* workers. Carelessness, sin, folly, sadly spoil our work.

As we get older, clay-modelling seems to get more difficult, because we see so much better what it ought to be. Faults we did not detect when we were younger now we see.

What shall we do? Give up clay-modelling? No, never. Try again. And if you can't make just the vessel you thought, make another, and by and by you will be able to make the one you desire most of all.

It is recorded of Wedgwood that he was trying to make an imitation of the Portland Vase in the form of jasper ware. In the soft clay the vases were done to perfection, but when they came out of the oven they were spoiled. This went on for six months. Then one of the workmen said to Wedgwood in despair, "Master, we have drawn the oven again, and we haven't got a single good vase." The master's reply was, "Well, you have had your wages, haven't you? *Go on.*"

They did go on, and shortly after, they succeeded, and the celebrated vase was produced.

> "If *you* don't succeed at first,
> Try, try again."

And then, when we have finished our clay-modelling, we shall be able to bring to God a character-vase which He will prize.

Be good modellers, boys and girls, and God will help you more and more.

A child once asked Charles Kingsley to write a song for her, and this was what he wrote—

> "My fairest Child, I have no song to give you;
> No lark could pipe in skies so dull and grey;
> Yet, if you will, one quiet hint I'll leave you
> For every day.
>
> "I'll tell you how to sing a clearer carol
> Than lark who hails the dawn or breezy down;
> To earn yourself a purer poet's laurel
> Than Shakespeare's crown:
>
> "Be good, sweet maid, and let who can be clever:
> *Do* lovely things, not dream them, all day long;
> And so make Life and Death, and that For Ever
> One grand, sweet song."

Hedge-Breakers

"Whoso breaketh a hedge, a serpent shall bite him."
ECCLES. x. 8.

SERPENTS hide away from you. They coil themselves up amongst the bracken and long grass; sometimes at the bottom of the hedge, or in a hole, or amongst the stones, you may see their bright eyes as they rest in the sun. The hedge of which the text speaks would be a stone wall, an old wall, the crannies of which are the favourite haunts of serpents, so that when men are engaged pulling such a wall down, they have to be careful lest a serpent bite them.

Amos speaks of a man going into his house, leaning his hand on the wall, and a serpent bites him. This would be a mud wall, ever liable to crack and break and not so compact as ours, where therefore serpents could lie.

I daresay, if you turned over the dry stone wall of any orchard or vineyard in Palestine, you would find snakes. And I know some boys who would love to hunt for them.

Our text speaks of the man who is taking down the old wall, and the serpent bites him. The hedge-breaker of the verse is the man who is trying to make things better in his city by pulling down some of the old abominations. He is what we to-day call a Reformer. Now the writer warns him that "Whoso breaketh a hedge, a serpent shall bite him." If he tries to pull down the old hedge and put a better one in its place, he must not wonder if he suffers.

And in that sense the text has something to say to boys and girls well worth their hearing. We must try and do all the good we can, and whenever we find out any evil, pull it down and put good in its place. But old evils, like old walls, have many nasty things in them that bite.

If, for instance, you find cheating going on in the class or on the playground, and you do your best to stop it, and get everyone to do the right, you won't find it easy. Some may call you nicknames, others may try to get you into trouble.

But we must not give up because good-doing is difficult. Some of those who have served their country most nobly have suffered most.

But it is another kind of hedge-breaking that I want to speak to you about. He that breaketh through a hedge, *when he ought not*, a serpent shall bite him.

God has put *three hedges* about our life, which we are liable to break through.

1. *The Home Hedge.*

The law of mother and father is like God's fence

about our life. The rule of home, which says we must not go out without leave, and must come in at a certain time; which sends us to bed, and makes us get up; which decides what friends we shall have, and the kind of games we shall play,—all this is God's hedge about our child life.

We don't always like the hedge, and are often tempted to break through it. If ever any of you should be so tempted, remember the text.

This incident was sent to me from America recently:

There is in the State prison at Stillwater, Minnesota a young man sentenced to a life imprisonment. His parents were cultured Christian people who possessed abundant means, and Charles was educated in the best colleges our country affords.

"After graduating from Johns Hopkins University, he wanted to perfect his knowledge of chemistry and went to the University of Berlin for that purpose.

"Charles had always been a wayward boy, and while abroad, fell in with a wild set of young men. With his impulsive nature, it was hard to withstand temptation, and he soon drifted from bad to worse. On his return to America, his parents were nearly heartbroken at the change, and the mother died soon afterwards.

"One day, in a drunken frenzy, he committed a crime that brought the punishment stated above.

"Not long ago, in conversation with him, a friend asked him what he considered the first step that led him to the downward road. This was his reply:

"'Nothing more or less than disobedience to my parents.'"

2. *The School Hedge.*

School is the place of discipline, learning, and sport Its laws are punctuality, obedience, industry. We must not copy, must not cheat, must not play at work and ever so much more, well known to all schoolboys and girls. "What's the use of it all?" we sometimes say. It is a hedge about our life, helping us to get knowledge and become wise, and be successful in the world. Don't break through it. Playing truant cheating, laziness, these are hedge-breaking; and a serpent will bite us.

3. *The Conscience Hedge.*

A boy, going home through the fields on a hot day, was lounging round a pond, when at the side he saw a frog sitting up as still and quiet as frogs only sit. His bright eyes were shining in the sun, which Mr. Frog was evidently greatly enjoying. The boy had a stick, of course, and as he saw the frog's head, a tempting target, up went the stick to strike. While, like the golf-player, he was taking aim, something within him said, "Don't, don't," and he didn't. Why indeed should he hurt the helpless, harmless creature? At home he told his mother, asking her, "What was it that said, Don't"? She replied, "Well, my boy learned men call that 'conscience,' but I call it *God's*

Voice. It will often speak to you. If you pay attention to it, the voice will grow clearer, but if you do not regard and obey that voice, it will gradually leave off speaking to you, and leave you to go your own way."

Yes, it is just so, boys and girls. Keep this hedge, and it will fend us from wrong, and help us to do right. Break through it, and the serpent will bite us.

And serpents' bites are cruel, deadly things.

Let us make this our rule, never to break through the hedges of our life. And when we are old, we shall be thankful and glad.

Wood=Gatherers

"The children gather wood."
JER. vii. 18.

WHO hasn't seen the stick-gatherers in the country or in the woods near town. Women with aprons full, children dragging fallen branches, and with arms full of sticks, and sometimes men with sacks filled to the top.

Ever since sticks fell, people have gathered them, When Elijah met the poor widow who had only a handful of meal left, and a very little oil in the house, she was gathering sticks. And so poor was she, and her requirements so small, that she said she was "gathering *two sticks*," meaning a very small quantity (1 Kings xvii. 12).

You will remember about one stick-gatherer who went about his work on a Sunday, and what befel him (Num. xv. 32).

So our text speaks of a far-away day, when, in the worship of the "Queen of Heaven," the children were the stick-gatherers. The people had become wicked and idolatrous, and they thought they would have good harvests and plenty of grapes if they could be on good terms with the deity represented by the sun and the moon, so they worshipped the sun as Baal, and the moon as "Queen of Heaven."

In this latter worship they offered sweet cakes made round like the full moon, and covered with lights. These cakes were burned in her honour. There were three things in the preparation of the cakes—the sticks, the fire, and the dough. The fathers made the fire to cook the cake, the mothers kneaded the paste, and the children gathered the wood for the fire. Thus father, mother, and child each had their share in the preparation for the worship of the "Queen of Heaven."

It is very rarely that in the religions of the world there is any place for children. A sorrowing mother in China brought her little girl to the missionary, and asked him to take it. He asked her why, and her reply was, "Because yours is the only God who cares for children."

There is much truth in that: the religion of Christ is the religion of childhood as well as of men and women.

Let me ask you to learn from these young wood-gatherers.

1. Children may be Christ's *worshippers*. In the worship of Christ, far nobler and happier than that of the "Queen of Heaven," the young are found.

Christ loves our friendship, our love, our adoration, and our prayer. He is so gentle and good, His service is so simple, that we need not wait until we are men and women before we become His sincere worshippers.

Christ has sympathy with the thoughts and joys of

our childhood. And from our earliest life we have something within that responds to Christ.

In Sunday school a teacher asked her class how soon they thought we might give our hearts to God. The answers were many, and all mentioned some particular age (ten, nine, twelve, and so on), except one, and her reply, by far the truest and best, was—

"*As soon as we feel that we are sinners, and know who God is.*"

At whatever age that knowledge comes, when we are three or four or five or six years old, we may become Christ's worshippers.

We belong to Him even before we feel that we are sinners and know who God is. And if, immediately we come to feel sin, we acknowledge ourselves as God's, and trust in Him as our Saviour and Father, then we may be amongst His worshippers all our life.

Many of the best and most useful people in the world began to serve God for themselves very early.

Old Polycarp, who was martyred when ninety-five years of age, said he had served God eighty-six years.

Matthew Henry the commentator began to love God when he was not quite eleven years old.

Isaac Watts, the lovely singer, before he was nine; and Jonathan Edwards, the American philosopher and theologian, thought he began to love God before he was seven.

Let no boy or girl think that they are too young to be among Christ's earnest lovers.

2. Children may be Christ's *workers*. These children in Israel gathered the sticks for their queen.

We have no fire to make for Christ, but we can be His wood-gatherers in other and much brighter ways.

1. We can bring to Him our own *heart service*.

Our love and praise and prayer we can offer Him.

You sing sometimes—

> " Saviour, blessed Saviour !
> Listen while we sing,
> Hearts and voices raising
> Praises to our King.
> All we have to offer,
> All we hope to be,
> Body, soul, and spirit,
> Now we yield to Thee."

That is wood-gathering for Christ in a high and happy sense.

3. Doing *little things* for Christ.

Some of you are missionary collectors. That is like gathering sticks. Remember, as you go your round collecting, that each penny you get is like a stick gathered for Christ, which He will accept.

Then, better still, we may try to get others to love Christ, or help those who do love Him. Sometimes a tiny word from us amongst our schoolfellows and friends may make others think. And our faithfulness to Christ will certainly help others to be true to Him. If ever you help a little friend to find Christ, you will be in the most wondrous sense a wood-gatherer for Him.

Now, I am sure none of you would object to gather sticks for mother if she needed them. You would walk miles along the lanes and sides of the fields to bring home a good armful.

And why? Because mother has done so much for us, and we love her? Yes, that is true. But also because we ought to—it is our duty to help mother.

Much more will we be wood-gatherers for Christ. We can all do something for Him.

Once in a English shipyard a large vessel was being launched. The wedges had been knocked away, but the ship did not go. Amongst the many who were trying to get the ship to move was a boy. Someone in the crowd laughed at him. His reply was, "I can push a pound." Quite so, and that was worth doing.

I remember, when I was a boy living by the seaside, helping the boatmen to pull up their pleasure-boats. No. 14 was my favourite. I couldn't pull much, but I did my best, and the skipper of the boat one day gave me a free sail. I put in my pound, and that was better than nothing.

If we cannot gather as much as some do for Christ, let us all do what we can.

"The children gather wood."

A Chance Arrow.

"And a certain man drew his bow at a venture, and smote the king of Israel between the joints of the harness."—1 KINGS xxii. 34.

WHEN Ahab, king of Israel, conquered Benhadad the king of Syria at Aphek, he spared him on condition that he would give up all the cities which his father had taken. But Benhadad failed to keep his promise, so far as Ramoth-Gilead was concerned. Hence, when Jehoshaphat, king of Judah, was visiting Ahab, he promised to help him take Ramoth-Gilead. With their combined forces they marched against Benhadad. Ahab, fearing that his enemy would make a mark of him, disguised himself, that is, took off his royal robes and went into the battle as a common soldier, while Jehoshaphat went in his own robes. The Syrian king did exactly what Ahab thought he would. He told his captains to fight with no one, small or great, save only with the king of Israel, thinking, I suppose, that if he could kill the king, he would easily conquer the subjects. The captains saw Jehoshaphat with his royal robes and said, "Surely this is the king," and turned aside to fight against him. **Then Jehoshaphat** made it known that he was not Ahab, so they ceased pursuing him.

Search as they would, these thirty-two captains could not find the man they wanted, upon finding whom the battle was to turn. Then one of the soldiers, taking aim at one of the enemy, draws his bowstring to his ear, and away flies the arrow. He hits the man he was aiming at, taking him as a common soldier. The arrow pierced through at the joints between the breastplate and lower armour, and brought down, not a common soldier, but the King of Israel.

Thus, what the captains with their special commission failed to do, this non-commissioned man did.

In our words and deeds we are often like this Syrian soldier, shooting chance arrows,—arrows well aimed at something, but striking a target we had not expected.

1. It is often so in the *things we do*. Some of the greatest consequences come out of the smallest deeds.

There is a boy blowing soap-bubbles, as I suppose we all have done. He thought of nothing much but the beauty and size of the bubble, and how long it would last before it would burst. But Newton, the great philosopher, watched him, and was helped to some of his most important discoveries in optical instruments. Yes, much may come even out of our bubble-blowing.

When the Danes were invading Scotland, they prepared for a night attack on the sleeping garrison. When near, they crept along barefoot, and had almost reached the spot, when one of the Danish soldiers stepped on a great thistle, which made him cry out. The cry aroused the sleepers, and all sprang to arms, with the result that the Danes were driven back.

I believe that the idea of printing was first suggested by a man cutting his name in the bark of a tree, and then getting an impression of it on paper which he placed over it.

You will all be able to recall many other instances of the same fact, that often the small chance deeds of life work the greatest results. The most important arrow of all shot on this battlefield was the one of our text, and the archer thought nothing about it.

These chance arrows are shot by us when we are doing things about which we say, "Oh, it's *no use*." If anyone had told this man of our text that he might likely shoot the king and win the battle, he would have laughed at the idea and said, "Not I."

We often can't see how we can do a particular thing, and therefore don't try. Some of those who have won the greatest distinction in school, when they began would have said, if questioned, "It is not much use for me to try, I am not clever." Never mind, shoot the arrow you have got, and who can tell what it will lead to.

When we say about something, "it doesn't matter," we may be shooting an arrow which will matter very much. The boy cheating at marbles, the girl careless about her friendships, the young man giving up church-going, and a host of others, say, "Oh, it doesn't matter." But the arrow hits a mark we did not expect.

A brother and sister were strolling through a field and came upon a nest of rabbits. The sister was delighted with the pretty little things, but the brother laughed at her, seized the rabbits, tormented them, and then threw them up in the air, letting them fall and kill themselves. He enjoyed this cruel pastime, though his sister besought him with many tears not to do it. Ten years afterwards he was hung for shooting a farmer, while poaching. He said to his sister, almost heartbroken, "Do you remember the nest of rabbits ten years ago, how you begged and prayed, and I ridiculed? I verily believe that from that day God forsook me, and left me to follow my own inclinations. If I had yielded to your tears then, you and I would not be weeping these bitter tears now."

What did a rabbit matter? But the cruel deed mattered everything.

2. We are often like this soldier in *the words we speak.*

We say perhaps a wrong word without thinking about it, and our younger brother hears and never forgets it.

The unkind word escapes our lips without any purpose in our heart to really hurt anybody, but it goes like a poisoned arrow into another heart.

It is just as true of the good words of our life.

The minister prepares carefully what he wants to

speak to the people, but it is sometimes the unprepared word that does the good. One who had very joyously found Christ said to her minister afterwards, in explaining it to him, "It was that word 'trust' that did it." He would not have thought of that chance word being the helping one.

Shoot all the chance arrows of kind, helping words you can, for you never know what they may do.

A lady bought a paper of a ragged, dirty newsboy, and with a smile dropped a few extra pennies into his sooty hand, saying, "Buy you a pair of mittens; aren't you cold?" He replied, "Not since you smiled."

So even a smile may be like a chance arrow, carrying not death, but joy and cheer.

Let us learn, boys and girls, from our Syrian soldier, that there are really no unimportant deeds or words.

A deed is great not always in itself, but in what it accomplishes. And those we think the least of are sometimes the most serious. Therefore, be careful about the chance words and deeds.

Little by Little

"He that is faithful in a very little is faithful also in much."
LUKE xvi. 10 (R. V.).

IF we mind the greater things of life, avoiding the evil and doing the good, we think that the smaller things will take care of themselves, and we shall be good. But it is not so. If you saw a man putting his cart before the horse, and yet expecting to go the way he wished, you would say, "What a foolish man!" But that is what we do when we think that big things are important, and little ones don't matter. Christ says if we are faithful in very *little* things, we shall be faithful in great ones.

How do we come to write well? We don't begin by making sentences, or words, or even letters. Our first work is in straight lines (which are often anything but straight) and "pothooks," then letters, then words, and then sentences. And after all this, many people manage to write what very few can read, because they are not faithful in the little things of writing.

And so it is in duty and character. We learn to do well, and we become good by fidelity in the very little things.

We look forward to the time when we shall be men and women, with our own purse and watch, and when, as we think, we shall be our own master. But these are not the most important and enjoyable things. The greatest thing is, that we are honourable men and women, for without honour all else will be vain. Christ's saying is to teach us how to become honourable.

Now let us think about this.

1. In those qualities which make character, we must be faithful in very little.

No one has good character who is not *truthful* Liars are made by carelessness in very little things. They begin by telling half truths, or by keeping silent when they ought to speak, or by acting little lies, as when a boy puts his hymn-book before his face, his lips moving as if he were singing, while yet he is talking to his neighbour. A schoolboy once said to his master, " I never didn't do it." He knew that two negatives make an affirmative, and thought the master wouldn't detect his deception. Of course he did, and gave him double strokes for the two negatives.

Truth is built up by care in the smallest things.

Two boys stood side by side in the market, one selling melons and fruit, the other selling oysters and fish. Boy A had sold out all but one large melon, when a customer came admiring it and asking the price.

"The melon is the last I have, sir, and though it looks very fair, there is an unsound spot on the other side." The gentleman declined the melon, and, turning to boy B, said, "Are those oysters fresh?"

"Yes, sir, fresh this morning,"—meaning that they were put on his stall that morning. A purchase was made. Then, turning to his friend, he said—

"What a fool you were to show the gentleman that spot in the melon! He would never have looked at it until he had gone away."

"I would not," said the other, "tell a lie, or act one either, for twice what I have earned this morning. Besides, I shall be better off in the end, for I have gained a customer and you have lost one."

The gentleman never went to the fish-stall again, but was a regular customer of the fruit-boy's.

All true men honour truth, and we shall become truthful men and women by being "faithful in very little."

This is the way also concerning *honesty*. Thieves are not made all at once, they begin in littles. If you knew the history of many dishonest men, who lose their positions in later life, you would find that as children they had not been faithful in little things.

He would steal first from his mother's cupboard, saying, "It's only a biscuit, and it's mother's"; then he would purloin marbles from his schoolfellows; then, when change was given in excess, he kept it instead of taking it back; then, when out in the world, he took greater things, and—you know the rest.

2. There are two respects in which Christ's saying

should be remembered by us, so far as *duty* is concerned.

We must obey God, but unless we have learned to obey one another and our parents, we are not very likely to obey God. You may be sure that he who breaks his mother's law will break God's too.

We hope to get to heaven, to enjoy its pleasures and know its friends. But unless we are faithful in the things of earth, our chance of heaven is very small. Do you think God will give us the things of the Better Life, if we have spoiled the things of this? There are many passages which teach us that the award of heaven will be given according to our use of earth.

I have known people very fond of attending religious meetings and singing hymns, who were very unkind and unjust to their friends.

They forgot that he who is "faithful in very little, is faithful also in much."

So, boys and girls, if we are wise, we shall work from the little things to the greater ones, knowing that if we take care of the pence, the pounds will take care of themselves.

A friend once saw Michael Angelo at work on one of his statues. Some time afterwards he saw him again, and said, seeing so little done, "Have you been idle since I saw you last?"

"By no means," replied the sculptor. "I have retouched this part and polished that; I have softened this feature and brought out that muscle; I have given more expression to this lip, and more energy to this limb."

"Well, well," said the friend, "all these are trifles."

"It may be so," replied Angelo; "but recollect that trifles make perfection, and that perfection is no trifle."

If we work thus in trying to be good and to do right, we shall complete our work, noble in God's sight, and He will say, "Thou hast been faithful over a few things; I will set thee over many things; enter thou into the joy of thy Lord."

Mimics

"Imitate not that which is evil, but that which is good."
3 JOHN 11 (R.V.).

THERE is in nature what is called mimicry,—the copying of something else. A little fellow brought to me a sprig of gooseberry, and asked me if I could find a caterpillar on it. Expecting some very little rogue to be somewhere on the leaves, I gave it up. But there it was, an inch and a half long, stretched from one twig to another, just the colour and size and shape of the gooseberry stem, and quite as motionless. It was a mimic.

In the Natural History Museum, South Kensington, there is a case with many of these mimics in. There are stick insects: long, lean things with strange legs, looking exactly like the twigs on which they stand; butterflies, with the upper side of their wings beautifully coloured, but with the under side (that which, when they rest, is visible) almost exactly like the leaves on which they alight, so that their enemies shall not see them; moths, with their hind-wings brilliantly coloured, so that they are visible in flight, but with their fore-wings much the colour of the bark of the tree which they frequent, because they rest, not with their wings upright as the butterflies do, but folded down like a roof; butterflies and moths of one species like those of another whose colours are a protection for them against their foes.

So animals will copy one another. One going a particular way, all will follow. A flock of sheep were going down a street. One of the foremost came suddenly upon a doorstep and jumped to get out of its way, and then all the following sheep jumped, though few of them were anywhere near the step.

I said to a child who was laughing, "What are you laughing at?" "Nothing," was the reply. Why do you think she laughed? Because others were laughing, though she did not understand why.

Yes, there is in all of us a wonderful power of mimicry, of making ourselves like other people. Indeed, I think, we are nearly all of us just a copy of someone else.

Now good, kind John tells us what sort of mimics we are to be; what we are to imitate.

1. Not *that which is evil.*

We shall scarcely ever know anyone in whose life there is not some imperfection or some evil. Never copy it.

The funny thing is, that we are all more inclined to copy the evil than the good. We are more drawn to imitate the scholar who comes late to school than the one who is always in time.

Slang words, bad words, idle words are much oftener copied than good words.

To some natures cruelty is more attractive than kindness, so that, for one who will protest against bullying the small boy who can't knock his bully down, there are twenty who will approve.

Perhaps evil is easier than good; and if so, that is one reason why we should not follow it.

It seems more manly and courageous to imitate evil. Little boys think that it looks quite big to have a small pipe in their mouth. But it isn't at all big, it is only very foolish. I only know one other creature which looks quite as foolish, and that is a monkey dressed up in boy's clothes, with a man's pipe in its mouth.

No, there is nothing brave or wise or manly in imitating that which is evil. St. John says, Don't do it. And we can understand why: because we become what we copy. A boy copies the ways of bad boys, and he becomes a bad man. Our mimicry becomes a part of ourselves; so that if people don't know our copy, they think that it is our own real self that they see.

2. But *that which is good*.

There is much we may and should copy. We acquire the best parts of our character by imitating the good points of others. Find out the good and follow it.

If you see a boy who will rather be laughed at and mocked than disobey his mother, imitate him.

If you find a girl who will go with one pleasure less, that someone else may have one, copy her.

If you see a boy who will rather lose his place in class than tell a lie, follow him. Or if you know one who, when he left home, said his prayers, though all in the same room ridiculed and pelted him with slippers and pillows, imitate him.

Wherever you find gentleness, truth, sincerity, kindness, goodness, or suchlike, imitate it.

We learn to do our best things by copying. Some of you like painting. Now, how will you become a good painter? By carefully copying good things, either from nature or from other pictures.

And so very largely do we become good and noble.

There is a beautiful verse in St. Paul to help us in this copying work of ours. He said once to the Corinthians, "Be ye imitators of me, even as I also am of Christ" (1 Cor. xi. 1).

We are to imitate others, so far as they are like Christ. We have noble lives about us: boys and girls at school who are above mean and dirty things; people who love Christ tenderly. Let us try to be like them. But, most of all, Christ Himself is to be our copy. Imitate Him.

Tradition says that when King Wenceslaus of Bohemia was going, one bitter winter's night, to the church in which he worshipped, the little page who followed him began to faint and fall. The king, hearing his cry and learning his difficulty, called out to him, "Put thy feet into my footprints, and all shall be well." The boy did so, and all was well.

Put thy feet into Christ's footprints, and all will indeed be well.

"Be ye imitators of God, as beloved children." Avoid bad company, wrong words, evil deeds. Try to copy that which is good, especially those who are good, more especially Jesus Christ, who has nothing in Him not to be copied, and who will Himself help us to copy all that He was.

A Good Copy

"Be ye imitators of me, even as I also am of Christ."
1 Cor. xi. 1 (R.V.).

In our last sermon we were talking about mimicry, how we all imitate others, and how much our life is made by what we thus imitate.

But there is another lesson for us to learn; namely, that while we are all copying somebody, somebody is copying us. That we are not merely copiers, but copies.

I don't know how soon we become such, but it must be very early. Perhaps you are, say three years old, but the baby of the home will copy you—your voice, your manners, your noises. How soon the little child will repeat the tone of the street cries, or the shake of your head, even before she can speak one word.

And so older ones are always copies for younger ones. The great responsibility of being the older sister or brother in the home, the senior girl or boy in the school class, is that the younger ones will copy us.

But it doesn't always go by age. Older ones often copy younger ones; and the older people get, the more inclined they are to copy the good things even in the youngest.

Strong ones are copies for the weaker. The dux of the class, the best athlete in the school, the leader in games, these stand out prominently as copies for others.

So that we all come in and belong to the class of those who are being copied.

The great thing is to be a good copy. We know the importance of this in music and painting and writing. No teacher would place before us an indifferent writing example to copy. It is very important, if we are to have a good "hand," the style we learn from should be good.

So it is in our life: the important thing is that our influence should be good; that when others copy us, they shall be the better for it, and not the worse.

This is what Paul speaks of in the text—"Be ye imitators of me, *even as I am* of Christ." "Try to be like me: try to do as I do in the world of men, try to mimic the example of my life."

He felt that Christ was so much to him, and had so influenced his character and moulded his conduct, that so far he was a good copy for others. He could read the writing of Christ on his heart and life. He did this in many ways, but when he wrote these words, he did it in two ways. First, Christ had given him a new and wonderful consideration for others. "I please all men, not seeking my own profit, but the profit of the many, that they may be saved."

He laid out his life for other people, not simply to help their pleasure and happiness, but to further their higher interests in salvation, that they might escape from their sins, and love God.

Christ saved him from selfishness and from forgetting the *best* interests of others.

And secondly, Christ had given him a new zeal for God. "Do all to the glory of God."

He tried to remember God in all he did and said, and the honour or dishonour he might bring to His name.

Thus, in love for men and zeal for God, in which he was a follower of Christ, he felt that he was a good copy for others.

This is the way still to make our lives worth imitating. Let us copy Christ, and then we need not fear others copying us. Let us do our level best to make ourselves as beautiful, as helpful, and as cheering as we can to others.

I will mention only one consideration which should urge up to this.

Think how much good we may do if we are good copies.

By a word or a deed we may injure a boy's or a girl's whole life, or (and this is the bright side) we may be of lifelong worth to it.

"This," says the headmaster of Harrow School, "is the service which every true boy renders to his school. Not that he does something or says something, but that he *is* something which all other boys may wish to be.

> 'The greatest gift the hero leaves his race
> Is to have been a hero.'"

That is his one imperishable benefaction, and there is none that can ever divest him of it. The whole spirit and tone of a cricket eleven may be changed and made splendid by one good fellow in it.

Many a brother has been kept from evil by the remembrance of his sister.

Many a little fellow down at heart has been cheered into new deed by the example of his schoolfellow.

Dr. Newton tells of two boys who slept together. One of them had been trained to kneel down every night before getting into bed, and say his prayer in an audible voice, and to repeat a text of Scripture which his mother taught him.

The first time he slept with the other boy, who never said any prayers, he was tempted to jump into bed, as his companion did, without praying. But he thought that would be cowardly and mean, and said to himself, "I am not afraid to do what my mother taught me; I am not afraid for anyone to know that I pray to God. I'll do as I have been taught to do." And he did. When both had become old men, he who as a boy had not prayed, sent for his old friend, as he lay on his deathbed, to come and see him. He had for years now been serving God, and he told his friend that it was his prayer and text so faithfully said every night, when they were boys together, which led him to become a Christian. He repeated the prayer and verse, word for word, and with his dying lips thanked him for his example, for that had saved his soul.

That is being a good copy, which others, following, may find their way to God, and have life made noble and happy.

Remember, boys and girls, that we cannot be what we are without influencing others for good or ill. Let us try never to do anything which would injure others, if they imitated us. This is the question we may ask ourselves, "What sort of a copy am I?"

And if only we love Christ and seek to do His will, we need have no fear in asking the question, because He will write some of His own letters on our life.

The Door

"Jesus said . . . I am the door of the sheep."
JOHN x. 7.

How important the door is! What would a house be without one? Did you ever know a builder build such a house? And how important that the door should open when necessary! Perhaps some of us have come home and found the door fast, while we had no key to open it: what trouble then!

And equally important, too, that it should be closed when necessary. I heard one night the house bell ringing, and then the step of a man in the hall, and then his voice call, "Hallo! anyone there?" I soon let him know that I was there, and wanted to know who he was and why he was there (though I had a shrewd guess who it was). "You have left your front door unfastened, sir," said the constable. Ah! that does not do in places where thieves come. There are times when it is as important for the door to be fast as that at other times it should open.

Now, Jesus said, "I am the door of the sheep." Not, you see, a house door, but the fold door for the sheep.

The Eastern sheepfold is walled round with a high wall, hence the necessity for a door.

There are two things about this door we should consider.

First, the use of the door.

"By Me," said Christ, "if any man enter in he shall be saved, and shall go in and out, and shall find pasture."

(*a*) The door is the *way in*.

After the day's feeding, the shepherd brings home his sheep, so that for the night they may rest safely in the fold. He could not leave them in the wilderness (the pasture ground) or on the hillside because of wild beasts, such as wolves and lions, that prowl about, and robbers that steal. Hence the Eastern shepherd carried a staff or crook, with which he guided and encouraged his sheep, and also a club (called "rod" in the shepherds' Psalm, the 23rd) with a spiked head, by means of which he drove off wolves and robbers.

And hence the need of the walled fold, that the sheep in peril from many foes may be safe and enjoy their rest.

We are like sheep with many enemies, and Jesus is our door into safety. Sin is like a hungry wolf—Satan is like a robber.

A small boy came one day very earnestly to his father with this queer question: "Father, is Satan bigger than I am?" "Yes, my boy," said the father.

"Is he bigger than you, father?"

"Yes, my boy, he is bigger than your father."

The laddie looked much surprised and very thoughtful, and then asked—

"Is he bigger than Jesus?"

"No, Jesus is bigger than he is," answered the father.

"Then," said the little fellow, with a smile, "I am not afraid of him."

We need not be afraid of any, because we have perfect safety through Jesus the door.

(b) The door is also *the way out*.

In the morning the shepherds call their sheep and lead them out to pasture—beside the "waters of rest and the pastures of grass."

So Christ says, "By Me they shall go out and find pasture."

Mr. Wells says: "A sultan once promised to spare the life of his enemy if he gave up his sword. When the disarmed warrior asked for food, the sultan replied, 'I promised to save your life, but not to feed you,' and left his prisoner to die of starvation."

Unspeakably mean, was it not? Christ does not simply protect us from our enemies—He feeds us also. He is the door to safety, to abundance, and to rich pasturage. All our souls need, Christ gives. So that our life is satisfied. Do we need help for duty? He gives it. Joy to make us glad? He gives it. Pleasure to brighten life? He gives it.

He satisfies all our desires. Boys and girls must

not think that Christ's service is all giving up things we like: it is receiving all that makes life good and glad.

Think of a sheep without any food or any drink! That is what life is like without Christ.

Christ is not the door to sadness and misery and tears, but to everything that is rich and good in life. When we speak of anyone "going in and out" of a place, we mean that they have the free use of it. If they want to go in, they can, or if they wish to go out, they can.

So Christ is the way "in and out" to safety and abundance. Whenever we are in fear, we can find safety in Him; or hungry, we can find satisfaction without any hindrance. We may be at home with Christ, so as to go in and out at pleasure.

Secondly. Now one word about our *using the door.*

Who may use the door? A door is not made for just anyone. It is made to let in and out all who ought to use it, and keep out all the rest—" the door *of the sheep.*" If Mr. Wolf comes, even with a sheep's skin on his back, he won't get through. The door is closed fast to the wolf.

If we are wicked and don't care about Christ, the door won't be open for us. But if we wish to be good, **to give** up our sins; and if we trust in Christ to save **us from** our sins and to feed us, then the door opens wide.

To everyone, to anyone who comes tired, sorrowful,

and needy to Christ, the door to salvation will immediately open.

What key opens it?

The golden key is trust. Trust Christ to be what He says He is, and He will be.

We use this key in prayer.

When you have done wrong, pray to be forgiven, and trust in Christ, and you will find that He delights in mercy. When you need help against temptation or in duty, ask and trust, and the help will be given.

There are some doors we could never open. Have you not seen large heavy doors that no child like you could move? Doors of learning, of wealth, of influence we may never go through, but the Door of Grace into Salvation opens to everyone who will trust.

"O Jesus, I will trust Thee."

Sides

"The Lord is on my side; I will not fear."
Ps. cxviii. 6.

WE all know what sides are. In many of our games the first thing is to get sides. And success depends very largely on who is on our side. If we can get the best bowler or the best bat in the cricket match, we think we shall win. I can well remember, as a schoolboy, how anxious we were to have the first choice when making a side.

This is true all through our life. The joy and worth of home are made by those who are on our side. To have everyone in the home against us would be sad indeed. When we are wanting anything very much, and can say, "Mother approves," we are a long way towards getting what we want, and we know it. I know some little girls who always try to keep father on their side.

What a difference it makes at school whether we feel that our teacher is for or against us. If we have been diligent and obedient, so that we are sure of her favour, we can do some very hard work without fear.

So there are sides in religion, in character-winning.

What we can become in goodness depends on who is on our side. In our contest against sin and trouble, the side on which God is conquers.

If we can say, when we are trying to be good and to do good, "the Lord is on my side," then we know that we shall succeed, and we may also say, "I will not fear."

Then *whose side is God on?* He is not on everybody's side in the same sense. There is a verse that says, "The face of the Lord is against them that do evil" (Ps. xxxiv. 16).

He is merciful to all, and will forgive whenever we turn to Him. But wicked people cannot say, "The Lord is on my side."

Who can say so?

1. All little children. We remember Christ's dear word, "Suffer the little children to come unto Me, for of such is the kingdom of heaven." When we have not learned to sin and to choose evil ways, we may be quite sure the Lord is on our side.

2. God is on the side of all who seek Him. We soon become conscious of sin in our hearts, but when we turn to God in confession and prayer and trust, we need not fear. A verse in one of the best known psalms says: "The sacrifices of God are a broken spirit: a broken and a contrite heart, O God, Thou wilt not despise" (li. 17).

This beautiful allegory was told by a dervish to a traveller in the East. "Every man has two angels— one on his right shoulder and another on his left.

When he does anything good, the angel on his right shoulder writes it down in his book and seals it, because good done is done for ever. When he has done evil, the angel on his left shoulder writes it down: he waits till midnight; if before that time the man bows down his head and exclaims, 'Gracious Allah, I have sinned; forgive me!' the angel rubs it out with a sponge; if not, at midnight he seals it, and the angel on the man's right shoulder weeps."

We shall never come to God through Christ, saying, " Gracious Father, I have sinned, forgive me for Christ's sake " but God will be on our side to pardon.

3. God is on the side of all who try to do right.

Whenever we are doing the best we can to be to others what we ought to be—for instance, a good sister in the home—to do to others what we should like them to do to us;

Whenever we are trying to conquer our evil tempers, —to be kind and gentle instead of rough and angry;

Whenever we are in a position that to tell the truth will cost us much, and we are therefore tempted to lie, but we are still resolute for the truth;

Whenever duty of any kind is difficult, but we try our best to do it;—

Then, in all these things and others like them, God is on our side to help and give us the victory.

When David was watching his flock, and a lion or bear came and carried off a lamb, he went after him, caught him by the beard, smote him and slew him, and delivered the lamb. We do not know how many lions and bears he thus slew, but it was not an uncommon experience for the shepherd youth. He never failed because God was on his side, and he knew it. Then when he came to the greater task of meeting Goliath, the mighty man of war, he did not fear at all, but said, "The Lord that delivered me out of the paw of the lion and out of the paw of the bear, He will deliver me out of the hand of this Philistine."

WHAT IS THE ADVANTAGE of having God on our side? "I will not fear."

It makes us bold and glad. I have heard boys say before a game, "We shall win, So-and-so is playing to-day."

God's is always the winning side, and if He is with us, we need fear no failure or foe.

The little blind girl holding her father's hand goes along through the crowded city street with its hundred perils, in perfect confidence. Why? Because of the one who is with her.

A tiny boy was sent upstairs to fetch something for his mother. He went out of the lighted room into the dark hall. The gas was not lighted either in the lower or upper hall. He felt a bit frightened at first, then up the stairs he climbed, saying to himself all the way, "Mamma loves me—she do!" He got back safely to his mother, and she asked him why he said those words over and over to himself as he went upstairs. "'Cause it helped me to get through the dark—that's why."

While his mother was there, and he was sure of her love, he did not mind so much.

So, God's love and presence being sure, we need not fear.

Let us all get on God's side, that we may all have Him on ours.

Secrets

"The secret of the Lord is with them that fear Him."
Ps. xxv. 14.

WE all know something about secrets, for who hasn't some to tell and some to keep? If you see two little heads close together, one pair of lips moving earnestly, and one pair of eyes looking very much interested, and helping the owner to listen attentively, and then you hear the speaker say, "You won't tell anybody, will you?" you know that a secret has passed between the two little heads.

Now our text speaks of God's secret, and those to whom He tells it.

1. What *God's secret is*.

God has a great many secrets which He keeps to Himself,—"It is not for you to know," He says,—but others which He tells.

The first is that of His love. The words in the verse really mean the love, the friendship of the Lord.

Love is always a secret. People whisper when they say anything about it. If you want to tell your mother that you love her, you don't shout it across the room, but you go close to her ear and say, "Mother, I want to tell you a secret." Then she listens, and you just say, "I love you," and she looks as pleased as if you had brought her ever so costly a present.

So in Jesus God is whispering to us, I—love—you, though a great many never hear this secret.

God tells us, by His Spirit in our hearts, the great secret of His love.

I daresay there are many secrets you would much like to know; but the best in all the world is this of God's love.

God has also secrets of grace to tell us.

He said to His people of old time, "I am thy God, I will strengthen thee: yea, I will help thee." We shall find this, too, when we need forgiveness because of sin. He will pardon. When we need help for our school work, or our playtime, in our sorrow or trouble, God will give it.

A poor little humpbacked boy was walking his weary way, his hands on his knees to help keep up his bent, burdened body. He passed by some boys playing marbles,—strong, straight, and gay they were. "Hey! I say, tell us who put the pack on your back? Here, let's carry it for you," said these cruel boys, while they caught hold of the cripple with the intention of carrying him, and having some fun. Could you think of anything more mean and cowardly? Boys and girls, never increase by taunt or deed the sorrow of those already sad enough by physical imperfection. The poor laddie twisted himself free from their cruel grasp, and turning his pale face on them with a look of dumb patience in his large, wistful eyes, he answered their taunting question and said, " God put it there, and *He helps me to carry it every day.*"

The boys slunk back to their marbles, and let him go on his way, to live out as best he could his crippled life, with this daily help of God. He had learned God's secret of help, which the boys at marbles knew nothing of.

God has secrets of happiness to whisper to us if we will listen.

We all like to be happy. I never knew anyone who did not try in some way to be happy. But sometimes those who try most are the saddest, because they go the wrong way to work. This boy thinks if he has plenty of cricket, and all else that he wants, he will be happy. This girl thinks if she has all the nice dress she desires, plenty of friends, and lots of parties, then how happy she will be!

But it does not follow. We may have all these, and not be happy. God teaches us the real secret of happiness. "Happy," said Christ, "are the pure in heart." Goodness is the truest and most lasting joy. Unless we are good, happiness won't be much for us.

Then, after this, our greatest joys may be found in helping others. The old legend says that a king who loved his boy very much, gave him everything he could to make him happy — pictures, toys, books; a lovely pony to ride, and a row-boat for the lake;

servants and teachers. Yet he was not happy. A magician came to the court one day, and promised for a large sum to make the prince happy. The price was agreed upon and paid. The magician took the boy into a private room, wrote something with a white substance on white paper. Then he gave the boy a candle, telling him to light it and hold it under the paper, and see what he could read.

He did so, and the white letters turned into blue ones, and he read—

"*Do a kindness to someone every day.*"

The prince tried the secret, and became the happiest boy in the realm.

Yes, for young and old, be good, do good, is the double secret of happiness.

2. *To whom* does God tell His secrets?

We don't tell ours to any or everybody, do we? Some, who can't keep a secret, tell theirs to a great many. We think we know what no one else does, and twenty other people are thinking the same. That isn't like secret-telling, is it? It is to one true friend we tell our secret. God does not tell His to just anyone —"the secret of the Lord is with *them that fear Him.*" To fear God does not mean to be frightened for Him, but to *obey* Him, to do what we know God wants **us to** do, and not to do what God disapproves.

To those who obey Him God tells His secret.

There is one thing in which God's secrets are unlike ours —**we** may tell them; He never says to us, "*Don't tell.*"

When Christ cured the two blind men and sent them away seeing, He told them that no one was to know it. But when they had got away, they could not keep the glorious secret, but spread abroad His fame in all the country. How difficult for them not to tell! Christ had special reasons for wishing to be quiet, but those reasons are past, and He lays no such secrecy on us. He says rather, "Go home to thy friends, and tell them how great things the Lord hath done for thee."

Not Mine—Whose?

"Ye are not your own; for ye were bought with a price."
1 Cor vi. 19, 20.

MINE and yours are two of the first words we come to understand. Having something of my own is one of life's first pleasures. At home we very soon come to have our own things; *my* toys, *my* books. Can any of you tell how soon you said with pleasure, "That is mine?" or how proud you felt when you could say, "I have a book of my very own?" I think one of the first hard lessons of baby life is to learn what is not theirs. Babies wish to have everything that they like, and don't know how much about "yours," if they do about "mine."

Then in our bigger life we have more and more to remember what is not ours.

And that is what our short text speaks about. First, what is not ours, and, secondly, why it isn't ours.

1. Not mine.

"Ye are not your own."

Just as everything belongs to someone, so does everybody.

The policeman, seeing a lost child crying in the street,

asks her, "What is your name? whom do you belong to?" Through many tears the little one replies, "My name is Dot, and I belong to mother." Quite right, though the answer doesn't help the policeman much. The wee child is only five years old, but she will belong to her mother just as truly when she is fifty. In a very happy sense we belong to one another, and so are not our own. But that is not what the text means. Not my own? Then whose am I? Paul says we belong to God.

Not mine, but God's.

People sometimes think that whatever else they have not, they have themselves, and they can do as they like with that.

"Eyes and ears, hands and feet, these anyhow are mine—can't I do what I like with them?" No, because we are not our own, but God's.

What a difference it makes whom we belong to!

Two boys were walking in the street together, engaged in very earnest talk, one doing nearly all the listening. The talker was telling his friend about his father—how kind he was, what long walks he took him, and what lovely things he bought him, and how many pennies he gave him. Presently the listener, quite overcome with this wonderful story, said, with a saddish tone in his voice, "I wish your father was my father."

Yes, it makes such a difference who our father is. It is good to belong to a good father, but it is better still to belong to God, and we all are His.

2. Why not mine?

We possess things in many ways. Sometimes they are *given* to us. "That is mine, it was given to me," we say.

Or we make a thing, and thus it becomes ours, "that is my boat, I made it myself." But we hear people say also, "That is mine, *I bought it and paid for it.*" Thus the thing is ours by purchase. So we are God's. "Ye were bought with a price."

What was the price? "Not with corruptible things, with silver or gold, but with precious blood . . . even the blood of Christ" (1 Pet. i. 18). Christ's life was the price paid.

By sin we have become slaves of sin, enemies of God, liable to punishment by the law of God. Christ gave Himself to God (especially on the cross), so that we might be again God's children. "Ye are not your own, for ye were bought with a price."

Christ paid the price for us. How good of Him! What do you boys and girls think of it? If a friend buys you something, you say, "How kind of her! I do love her." But she has only given money—Christ gave life and all.

On the 12th August 1893 there was a railway accident near Pontypridd in South Wales. Some were killed and many injured. Under the wreckage, in great danger of being crushed to death, was a boy who was rescued. When he was fairly out, and began to realise that he was saved, he looked gratefully at his rescuer, put his hand in his pocket and drew out a halfpenny and offered it to him, saying, "Please take this halfpenny, it's all I've got, and you do deserve it too."

The halfpenny was taken in remembrance of the gratitude of the lad, who received twopence in return.

What would you give to Christ because, in order to save us and make us God's children, He gave Himself? He wants our trust, our love, our obedience. And He "does deserve it too." Let us give it all, and He will give us back more than we give in joy, pleasure, and goodness.

In the old slave days, before Abraham Lincoln's slave emancipation, there was in the slave auction in New Orleans a beautiful mulatto girl put up. The bids rose from 500 dollars to 700, then a voice outside the crowd called 750 dollars. Higher and higher the bids went, until, at 1450 dollars, the stranger got the girl. He turned out to be a Northerner, and she hated the thought of becoming his slave. The next morning he called at the house where she was. She said sadly, "Sir, I am ready to go with you." "But I do not want you to go with me. Look over this," handing her the paper of her freedom. "I bought you that you might be free." She exclaimed, "You bought me that I might be free? Am I free? Free? Can I do as I like with myself?" He answered, "Yes, you are free." Then she said, with sobs of joy, "Oh, sir, I will go with you and be your servant for evermore."

There is perhaps not one of my boy and girl friends

who would not have said just the same. How much more should we promise Christ our lovingest service?

Let us remember, then, that we are not our own because Christ has bought us. We must let God have us.

If we took anything out of someone's house and did not return it, you know what we should be. And if we use our life as God does not wish, if we do not use all for Him because it is His, what then shall we be?

Let God have His own by living to love and serve Him. "Glorify God therefore in your body."

Alas! Borrowed

"Alas, master! for it was borrowed."
2 KINGS vi. 5.

THERE were schools in Israel established by the prophets for the teaching and training of the young men. During Elisha's life he used to visit them at regular intervals. There was one such school at Jericho, and when Elisha was visiting it on the occasion before us, the "sons of the prophets" (the students) said to him, "The place where we dwell before thee" (that is, the place where they assembled to hear his teaching—what we should call the schoolroom) "is too strait for us"; and so they asked permission to make a larger place. They wished to go to Jordan, about five miles distant, where in the valley plenty of trees were to be found, and there make it. The arrangement they suggested was that each man should cut a beam and carry it to the place of building. Elisha gave his consent, and was sending them off when they said, "Consent to go with us," and so the loved master went with them.

Such a school excursion as anyone might greatly enjoy! They had mostly to borrow their axes for the wood-cutting. And now they are at work. Merry work it is, for none of them understand tree-felling. Some get their beam off quickly, but here is one who has a tough one to chop at, and it does not come away. Swing, swing, goes his axe, and the chips fly. Then of a sudden away goes the axe-head, and with a great splash sinks in Jordan.

Elisha was near by, and the novice wood-cutter, looking at his headless handle, exclaimed, "Alas, my master! for it was borrowed."

The master was so sorry for his student that he went with him to the place and used the special power God had given him to recover the lost head. The iron rose to the stick the prophet threw into the water, and the young man took it and placed it again on the handle.

I like this young man's concern about the borrowed axe. He was troubled so much because it was borrowed. Let him teach us—

1. We have all many things *lent to us*. We soon become borrowers. Toys, books, and other things which we have not of our own, we frequently get others to lend us. But in more serious things we are borrowers.

Home, with its care, love, and many joys, is lent to us.

Our *name*, which we may honour or dishonour, is lent.

Most of all, *life* is God's great loan. Every day is like a polished axe-head lent by God, that we may do good work with it. School-days, play-days, work-days, are all lent.

Our *nature*, its power to love and to enjoy, to be good and to be evil, to think and to work, is lent to us.

The *world*, with its hills and valleys, trees and flowers, birds and butterflies, sunshine and shower, is also lent to us for a little time.

2. Borrowed things *have to be returned*. What you buy you may keep, but what you borrow you must give back.

If anyone lends you a house, you must leave it when the time is up in good condition. Or if one lends you a book, you must take it back when done with.

And this is very true of the great loans granted to us by God.

The home God has lent us must be returned by a faithful fulfilment of all its duties.

Days, when idleness fills them, are like lost axe-heads.

If we sin against our nature, we are neglecting to bring back to God what He has lent.

We are tempted sometimes to be careless with what is borrowed. I have heard little voices say, "Oh, it doesn't matter, it isn't ours." If the book were ours, we should cover it to take care of the binding, but because it is a library book, we don't mind.

Carelessness is the great destroyer of lent things.

3. Borrowed things *may be lost*. They get sometimes amongst our own, and we forget them.

By misfortune we may lose them. Look high and low and you can't find the borrowed toy. "Where can it be?" No one knows.

In both these ways we may lose God's lent things. We are so accustomed to home, to sunshine, to pleasure, that we forget God has lent them only.

We are also often like Elisha's student, who in using his axe, lost it.

Who does not know what it is to feel that after he has tried hard to use a day well, it has seemed at the end quite lost.

Lost things may be found. Elisha, out of his great sympathy for the student, helped him to find the lost head. How exciting the search must have been! I should like to have stood on the bank alongside of this boy, so grieved because of his loss, and seen him watch the up-coming of the iron. How glad he would be to have it securely in his hand again! The sorrow of losing was great, but the joy of finding was great also.

The more valuable the thing lost, the greater the joy when found.

There are always plenty of people to help us find the borrowed lost things. If we have lost any of our good name or character, there are many to help us regain it. When we say, "Come and help me find what I have lost," there will be no want of willing hands. And the one to help us most of all will be Christ.

Does it matter what we do with our borrowed things? Yes; to lose them finally will be sorrow, to bring them back will be joy. We can imagine this young man's delight when he returned,—perhaps to some cottager of whom he had borrowed the axe,—saying, " Here is the axe you lent me; I feared once I should never bring it back, but Elisha helped me, and here it is." So *we* shall have the approval of the one who has lent precious things to us.

A little newsboy in America, six years of age, was run over in the street. The poor little injured fellow cried for his mother. When she came, he said, "I've saved 'em, mother—I've saved 'em all. Here they are." In his clenched hands were ten cents.

Let us try to be like the newsboy over all that God has lent us.

If we can say to God, "I've saved 'em all," the day will be a very happy one to us when we see God.

Sparrows

(Matt. x. 29; Luke xii. 6.)

THERE are two sayings of Christ's about sparrows that are full of teaching and encouragement. Here is one—

"Are not two sparrows sold for a farthing? and not one of them shall fall on the ground without your Father" (Matt. x. 29).

This is the other—

"Are not five sparrows sold for two farthings, and not one of them is forgotten in the sight of God" (Luke xii. 6).

In the first saying, Christ refers to the catching of sparrows for sale.

However they are caught, whether struck by stick or stone, or taken in the net, Christ says, "Not one of them shall fall on the ground without your Father."

In Christ's country the little birds were generally netted, as they are in England to-day. I well remember as a boy seeing the linnet-catchers in Norfolk. They had a double net spread on the ground, which by means of a string they could pull over upon the unwary birds. In the midst of the ground, covered by the net, they had a bird tied by its leg to a stick which they were able to raise when they wished, and thus make the bird flutter as if flying. Then two or three songsters were placed near by, and groundsel was strewn about. Thus tempted birds on the wing would come down, and then the fowler would pull his net over them.

But, according to Christ's word, God knew and cared for each one thus taken.

In the other saying Christ refers to the cheapness of sparrows when sold, "five for two farthings" (perhaps about equal to our penny). The first text says they sold "two for one farthing." Those who could afford to spend a penny got one bird thrown in. Christ had seen these little creatures spitted on sticks—twenty on a stick—being sold in the marketplace to the poor people for food. I have no doubt He had heard the poor bargaining over them, and He said, "Not one of them is forgotten." Poor little dead cheap things, and yet God remembers each one.

We all love the birds. Spring and early summer owe much to them. The flowers would scarcely seem as beautiful if our bird friends were not here also.

But there are two things that I want you to notice about God's love of the birds. He loves the common ones, and each one.

First, God cares for the *common* birds—birds that are caught not because of their feathers or their song, but because they can be sold for food.

God knows and loves the birds with fine feather and delightful song, but he does not forget the dull-coloured, simple-voiced sparrow. And I think we can easily understand why this is so. The bird-life is not made up of colour and song merely, and the tiny life of the sparrow is as needy, as real, and as eventful as that of the rarer birds. God looks at the life, and therefore does not forget or neglect a bird because it is common.

Let us learn this. We think much about uncommon things. We like birds that are rare because they are few, or beautiful because of their gay feathers, or delightful because of their rich song. The peacock with his spreading tail, the kingfisher with his bright blue back, the nightingale with his full song, the blackbird with his loud morning call, the chiff-chaff with his delicate form and rousing "call to arms." All these and many more such we notice and love; but who cares for the sparrow, except to throw a stone at him? We ought to, for he would be greatly missed in town, and he too has his little life to live.

Those are the happiest and most useful people who have learned to prize the commonest things of life, and do well its most ordinary duties.

If also God cares for common birds, we may be sure He cares for common people. The rich, the clever, the good, God loves; but we cannot be so little, or dull, or poor, for God to forget us.

Secondly, God cares for *each sparrow*—" *Not one* is forgotten." I wonder how many sparrows there are in the world. God knows every one, and He cares for each. This is the way God loves and works. He does not love a crowd, but an individual. He loves all, by loving each; He feeds all, by feeding each one. This is true about ourselves. God knows not merely all boys and girls, but me. He loves all, but He loves *me*.

Let us, too, be like God as far as we can. We think much of great numbers, don't we? A *swarm* of bees, a *flock* of birds, a *crowd* of people, attract us. When we see the swallows assembling in late September or early October, before they migrate to their warmer home, we wonder at their numbers. But we care nothing for one.

The boy who keeps rabbits will see to them very attentively while he has many, but when only one is left, he forgets it. We say, " *Only* one."

We speak an unkind word and then say, " It was only *one*," or do a wrong deed, or go to a wrong place, and again we say, " Only *one*—only *once*."

God knows the worth and the power of one, and we must not forget. 1 beside 0 makes 10, while 1 away from the side of 0 leaves nothing. Wonderful little figure this one is!

Don't be careless about one word, or deed or habit. So Christ teaches us that God cares for birds, and common birds. Let us do the same.

Let country boys protect them during the nesting

season. Don't destroy their nests, or take all their eggs, or hurt their young; and persuade every boy you know to be kind to them in these respects.

Let girls do all they can to coax mothers not to buy little birds to put in hats, because they look very ridiculous, and their slaughter for this purpose is very sad and cruel.

Let neither boy nor girl throw stones at the birds, for they are God's, and He knows. Be one and all bird protectors.

A kind-hearted farmer who loved the birds had his reward in a wonderful manner. His little girl Patty wandered at harvest-time into the field where her father and his men were reaping corn. She saw them at the farther side of the big field, and tried to catch their eye, but could not, and so sat on a sheaf. Then a bird flew up out of the standing corn. She went to see if there was a nest, and found it with three little birdies in. Patty sat down in the long corn and talked to them. All the time the clicking machine with its sharp knives was coming on. And when near to where Patty was, the farmer said to one of his men, "Here, Tom, come and hold the team. There is a lark's nest somewhere near the old tree yonder; I will hunt it up, and you can drive round so as not to hurt the birds." Beside the nest he found his own bright little birdie; picked her up and kissed her, thanking God for the birds that had saved her. He might have thanked God that He had taught him to care for the birds.

Christ speaks of God's care for them, that we may be sure of His love for us. If God cares for sparrows, with their wee life and short history, how much more for us with our greater life.

Here are a few verses from "The Sparrow's Song," which beautifully express this—

> "I'm only a little sparrow,
>   A bird of low degree;
> My life is of little value,
>   But the dear Lord cares for me.
>
> . . . . . .
>
> I know there are many sparrows;
>   All over the world they are found;
> But our Heavenly Father knoweth
>   When one falls to the ground.
>
> . . . . . .
>
> I fly through the thickest forest,
>   I alight on many a spray;
> I have no chart or compass,
>   But I never lose my way.
>
> I just fold my wings at nightfall
>   Wherever I happen to be;
> For the Father is always watching:
>   No harm can happen to me.
>
> I am only a little sparrow,
>   A bird of low degree,
> But I know that the Father loves me.
>   Dost *thou* know His love for *thee*?"

Old Shoes and Clouted

"And old shoes and clouted upon their feet."
Josh. ix. 5.

If we had seen these men of Gibeon, with these old mended shoes on their feet, we should have said, "They have come so far that they have worn out their shoes on the road, and had to mend—clout—them!" And that is just the impression they wanted to make on Joshua and his people. The story is a very funny one.

Joshua had just begun his march into the Promised Land. He had taken two large cities and been most victorious. When the kings beyond Jordan heard of Joshua's successes, they gathered themselves together to fight. There were six kings with their armies. But the men of Gibeon thought they would try another plan. Rather than fight, they would get Joshua to make a covenant with them. To do this they must make him believe that they lived a long way off. And so they put old sacks on their asses, took wine-skins old and rent, old clothes, dry and mouldy bread, and old shoes and clouted.

Joshua was very suspicious of them, and said, But

perhaps you dwell among us; how shall we make a covenant with you?

And then they said all kinds of plausible things, and, pointing to their condition, said that they had taken their bread hot, and now it was dry and mouldy; their wine-skins were new, but now rent; and "our garments and our shoes are become old by reason of the very long journey."

Joshua said nothing to God about it, and made a covenant with them. Then at the end of three days he discovered the deception, and made them slaves for ever, to hew wood and to draw water for the house of God.

Boys and girls, never wear old shoes and clouted, to make believe.

All the lies do not come from the tongue: we may act a lie just as surely and easily as tell one, and we are as really liars when we do.

I knew a wood-seller who always carried two bundles of sticks, and said when he came to the door, "These are the last I have." But all the time he had a big sackful at the end of the street. That was "old shoes and clouted."

A boy asked a friend of mine for a penny, the exact sum he needed to buy a bat. So it was when he left home, but he asked twenty people for that penny, and got it.

A boy smoking sees his father coming: out comes the pipe, and into his pocket, and he meets his father as if he loved him, and were really the boy the father thinks him to be.

All this is like old shoes and clouted on our feet. Whenever we are pretending to be what we are not, or to be doing what we are not really doing, we are acting like these men of Gibeon.

Let me give four reasons why we should not make believe.

1. It is *mean*.

The schoolboy does not like to be called a sneak. He would far rather suffer a thrashing, or bear false blame. To make believe is sneaking. It is degrading both to ourselves and in the sight of others, and very unfair. If we are once found out, no one will trust us.

Aristotle, one of the great philosophers, was once asked what a man could gain by telling a lie, and he replied, "Never to be credited when he speaks the truth."

You may be sure that Joshua and his people would be pretty wary about the men of Gibeon, after their trick.

One of the saddest things that can befall us is to get the character of a deceiver, and therefore not to be trusted.

2. *It will out.*

Only three days, and their deception was discovered. Just a chance report came to Joshua that they had not come from a long distance, but were his neighbours and dwelt near to him. They had managed everything cleverly thus far, and then some person, unknown and unsuspected, "tells."

Yes, we can't hide much. In most strange and unexpected ways people find out when our old shoes are not genuine. Remember Gehazi. The wealthy Syrian captain was cured of his leprosy through Elisha, and pressed the man of God to receive a present. This he stoutly declined. Gehazi saw the Syrian go away with his treasures and chariots, and was greatly disappointed.

So, on the pretence that two young men had unexpectedly come from the hills, and his master would be glad of something for them, he ran after the "rich stranger" and asked for a talent of silver, and two changes of raiment.

Naaman gave him one talent more than he asked, and sent two servants to carry the present. This very much increased Gehazi's difficulty, lest his master should see these servants. So when they got to the hill, just before the house came into view he let them go, and he hid the present in some secret place; then he went over the brow of the hill, into the house, and stood before his master as if nothing had happened. How great his surprise when he found that all was known! Even the hill and his cleverness had not prevented the master knowing. "And he went out from his presence a leper as white as snow."

We shall be found out sooner or later.

3. *We* know, if no one else does.

A little girl in her Sunday school repeated the 23rd Psalm. A visitor who was present was so pleased with the way in which she did it, that he gave her a shilling. Great was the child's joy over the shilling, all her own. The visitor noticed this, and, guessing that she would spend it as soon as she could, said to her, "I see a great many shops open, though it is God's day. You must on no account spend that coin in any of them to-day, but keep it till to-morrow. You understand, I won't be present to see you, but there is One who will see you, and find out at once if you break the Sabbath day." The child was silent, her dark, thoughtful eye was turned up to the speaker's face as if she knew what he meant, and had taken it all in.

"Who will see you?" he asked, thinking he knew quite well what she would answer. "MYSELF WILL SEE ME," was her unexpected, but splendid reply. "Myself will see me." Do you think that would matter? Yes, very much indeed. It is terrible to hate oneself, to despise oneself, because—though no one else knows—we know that we have done mean and wicked things.

And, boys and girls, it comes to that sooner or later. We can bear the hate of others, if we know that we have done right, but the very love of our friends becomes a burden to us when we know that we have done wrong. The good opinion other people form of us is like a poisoned arrow when we know that we have deceived them. Don't make an enemy of yourself by wearing old shoes and clouted to make believe.

4. *God knows.*

When these men were getting together their old clothes, their rent bottles, their mouldy bread, and their old shoes, hoping, thinking, saying, "No one will know,"—someone knew.

When they inspected one another in their strange guise, and felt pleased with the effective display (for they looked just like men who had come off a very long journey), they did not remember that other eyes were there.

When they thought within themselves, "Surely we shall succeed: Joshua and his people won't find out," they forgot there was One who is "not mocked."

Brother and sister were carrying a basket of cakes to their grandmother. Nearly all children love cakes, and these two did. Presently they peeped through the half-open lid, to see what they were like. Then they opened it wide. Then they wondered what they would taste like, and they counted them carefully. "So many, we might eat one, just one, and no one will know. Perhaps mother didn't count them, and surely grandmother won't."

I rather think they would have eaten one, had not the sister asked a very awkward question—"Can't God count?" Down went the lid, and away the little folk ran to grandmother's.

Yes, that is it. God counts, and though no one else may know, and we "don't care," God knows, and to Him "lying lips are abomination," and so are lying feet.

When, then, you are tempted to act like these men with their old shoes, remember them and their fate, and be straight.

Lost Shields

"And he took away all the shields of gold which Solomon had made."
1 KINGS xiv. 26.

THERE is a very interesting history in connection with these shields. When Solomon was making his throne and drinking vessels and other wondrous things, he made also two hundred targets (shields large enough to cover the whole body), which he overlaid with gold, six hundred shekels going to each target. Besides these, he made three hundred shields, which he overlaid also with gold, giving about three hundred shekels to each shield.

He put these shields in his armoury, which he called "the house of the forest of Lebanon." He probably gave it this name because the pillars of the house came from the cedar forests of Lebanon. He used the shields on great state occasions.

In the fifth year of Rehoboam's reign, Shishak, king of Egypt, came against Jerusalem, and amongst other valuable things he took away "all the shields of gold which Solomon had made." The king made in their stead brass shields; and when he went to the house of God, the native troops carried them in state. But they were never like Solomon's costly shields; however they looked, they were but brass instead of gold. Here is a parable of life that we may learn together.*

Childhood gives to all of us golden shields of character to protect us against sin and temptation. If we keep our shields, we shall grow in goodness and beauty until we are "full-grown men in Christ." Trust, truthfulness, simplicity, love, obedience, happiness, are six of our most important shields.

But temptation comes; sin the great destroyer arises, and we are liable to lose them all. The history of some people from childhood to manhood is just a record of the loss of their shields. An artist who wanted a model of innocence saw one day a happy, bonnie boy playing by the stream side. That, said the artist, is Innocence. He coaxed the laddie to be his model, and painted him kneeling with his hands clasped in prayer, and got a very successful picture. Years passed away, and the artist became an old man. He had often thought he should like a companion picture, giving the other side of life—Guilt. He went to the prison and selected the most repulsive man there. His eye was that of a culprit, his countenance with lines of guilt which spoke of his degraded life. He served well the painter's purpose. When he came to question him about his history, he found, to his great surprise, that it was he who, as a lovely boy, had been his model of Innocence. Thus the artist had the two ends of life—the innocent, happy boy at the brook; the hard, debased man in the prison.

What had he done? Lost all his shields of character with which he began life,—truth, simplicity, honesty, obedience, happiness had all gone. But he need not have lost one. By trust in Christ, by prayer, by care, he should have kept them all.

Now let us look at some shields which we may lose but can keep.

1. *Simplicity* is like a golden shield.

As children we love the simple, the beautiful, the natural things. We have at first no "airs": foolish pride has not come to us. But as we grow older, we have to fight for our shield.

The tempter Pride comes to us, as we get to have things of our own, and to know the world so full of many vanities. Then, unless we keep our shield, we shall come to think much of ourselves because we know a little more than somebody else, or live in a bigger house than they. There will arise a great temptation (especially to my girl friends) to be vain about dress to think much more about what we put on than about what we are; to spend time on foolish dressing that we ought to spend in doing good to others.

I know nothing quite so foolish as the love of dress. How many I have known very sensitive about a pretty dress, but very forgetful of pretty deeds.

2. *Obedience* is another precious shield.

One of life's first and best lessons is this obedience. It seems irksome to carry, and we feel that we would much rather do as we like. But that would be a sad loss of shield. If we are to keep the law of our country, we must learn to keep that of home and school. If we are to do God's will, we must learn to do that of those above us here. If ever we are to rule truly, we must first learn to serve, for it is obedience that leads to all true kingship.

But this is one of the first shields stolen from us. We begin to feel that we are too big to obey. Big boys sometimes think it beneath their dignity to obey their mother. Then we soon make excuses: "What does it matter?" "No one will know;" "Just once;" and so we lose our shield.

3. *Truthfulness* is indeed a shield of gold.

There are some who do not know much about it, and others who do not care; but most of us begin life by feeling that we ought to tell the truth. We have a natural scorn for a lie. Nothing makes us so indignant as to be suspected of untruthfulness. To sneak is mean, but to lie is meaner.

Let us, at all cost, keep this shield. We are very liable to lose it. We are tempted not to be particular about *little* things; to tell only a half truth, to hesitate or prevaricate. When a lie would serve us, and perhaps save us some present trouble, we are in great peril of losing our shield. David did this once. He had just said good-bye to Jonathan and gone to Nob. Ahimelech the priest was afraid to see him alone, and asked him how it was. David was sorely pressed by hunger, and had no weapon. Then, in order to get bread and sword from the priest, he said the king had sent him on a secret mission. He got bread and Goliath's sword. But he lied, and in the loss of his shield endless trouble came: the priests were slain; Saul sinned; and David brought longer exile upon himself.

Never let anything rob you of your truthfulness. There is a beautiful story told of a mother in an Eastern land who sent out her boy to begin life in a distant city. She sewed inside his waistcoat forty gold dinars.

Her last counsel to him was to seek and to follow always the truth. On his way, he had to cross a part of the desert infested by robbers. One of these came galloping up and sternly asked, "Boy, what money have you got?" "I have forty gold dinars sewed up in my waistcoat." The Bedouin burst into a fit of laughter, thinking the boy was joking. Turning his horse, he galloped back to his troop. By and by a comrade came asking the same question, and, getting the same answer, he went back, thinking it a joke also. Then their leader came, and got the same answer. Leaping off his horse, he felt the boy's clothes till he counted the forty coins. "What made you tell the truth, my boy?" he asked. "My God, and my mother, sir," was the reply. Bravo, laddie! Did the robbers take his money? No, they let him go, and he prospered in the city whither he went.

So all our other shields may be lost. Envy and jealousy will rob us of love; selfishness and sin will take away joy; doubt and fear will destroy trust.

Let us ask *two questions.*

1. How can we keep our shields?

Be quite sure that we need not lose one. There is no necessity to be worse when we are old than we were when young. The sadness of these lines should not be ours—

> ". . . Now 'tis little joy
> To know I'm farther off from heaven
> Than when I was a boy."

By prayer, by care, and by faith in Christ as our Saviour and Friend, we shall keep our shields.

2. If we lose a shield, what then?

Rehoboam made brass ones instead of the gold. Shall we? No, we can win back the lost ones. By repenting of our sins, that is, telling God about them, and asking Him to forgive them; by consecration, that is, giving up our sins and giving ourselves to God, we shall win back the shields we have lost.

Never lose one; but, if you do, get it back quickly.

Apples of Gold

"A word fitly spoken is like apples of gold in baskets of silver."
PROV. xxv. 11 (R.V.).

THIS is a pretty verse, speaking to us about the importance of our words. "What does a word matter!" we often say. The wise man says it is—if fitly spoken—like an apple of gold in a basket of silver. By "apples of gold" the text does not mean apples made of gold, but golden-coloured fruit. You know that when people are writing poetry, they don't always call a thing exactly what it is, but name it from what it is like. And so, because of the rich colour and beauty of this fruit, the poet calls it "apples of gold"—meaning perhaps some kind of orange. Our poet sees this delicious fruit being carried in silver baskets, beautiful and valuable because of their metal and their chaste workmanship.

So that we have not merely rich fruit, but lovely baskets to carry it in. Fruit good to eat and pleasantly served.

"Words," says the poet, "fitly spoken," are like this golden fruit in the silver basket. What words could he mean?

1. Words which are fit *in themselves*—right words.

We may be quite sure that there are many words that are not like this, and have no silver basket.

Slang may be like the crab-apple, but it is not the golden apple. How out of place "crabs" would be in a silver basket.

Tale-bearing, slander, swearing are certainly not in our basket. Nor are careless words, spoken often only in jest. No; only right ones are like apples of gold.

A boy, the son of a poor labourer, was one day bowling a round stone in the road for fun. It struck against another stone in front of a cottage, rose up, and then crashed through the window. The man was at home, and very soon at the door to see who had done it. Finding the small boy in the road, he asked him whether he knew who had broken the window. What do you think he said—"That boy who has just run round the corner"? No, no, but like a man he answered, "I did, but I will pay for it," and then he told how it happened.

The cottager looked at him, surprised at his truthfulness, and said, "You shall not pay it all. You have neither run away nor told a lie, and although I am poor, I will bear half the loss myself."

The poor boy said words that were like **apples of gold** in a basket of silver.

Thus all true words, all kind words, **all words of repentance** and prayer, of sincerity and resolution, **of wisdom** and love, may be such as our text **speaks** of.

2. But the text means also right words said in a right way.

It matters much what we say, and much also how we say it. Kind words may be so roughly spoken that they lose all their kindness, and severe words may be so gently spoken that they do not sting overmuch.

When a black boy was asked by the missionary, "Who are the meek?" his reply was, "Those who give soft answers to rough questions."

We so often spoil words by speaking them wrongly.

A boy went to apply for a situation.

"Can you write a good hand?" the governor asked.

"Yaas."

"Good at figures?"

"Yaas."

"Know the city well?"

"Yaas."

"That will do. I don't want you," answered the merchant.

"But," said a friend when the boy had gone, "I know the lad to be an honest, industrious boy; why don't you give him a chance?"

"Because he hasn't learned to say 'Yes, sir,' and 'No, sir.' If he answers me as he did when applying for a situation, how will he answer customers after being here a month?"

So he lost the first situation he applied for because he hadn't learned about the worth of a word "fitly spoken."

Thus our text, with its beautiful picture of the golden fruit in silver baskets, teaches us the great worth of our words, when good themselves and when well said.

There is a short prayer which we should all pray—

"Set a watch, O Lord, before my mouth; keep the door of my lips."

Mind your words, boys and girls, and God will help you.

"Sir," said a lad coming down to one of the wharves in Boston, and addressing a well-known merchant—"Sir, have you any berth on your ship? I want to earn something."

"What can you do?" asked the gentleman.

"I can try my best to do whatever I am put to do," answered the boy.

"What have you done?"

"I have sawn and split all mother's wood for nigh on two years."

"What have you not done?" asked the gentleman, who was a queer sort of a questioner.

"Well, sir," answered the boy, after a moment's pause, "I have not whispered in school once for a whole year."

"That's enough," said the gentleman; "you may ship aboard this vessel, and I hope to see you the master of her some day. A boy who can master a wood-pile and bridle his tongue must be made of good stuff."

We could master the wood-pile; let us try also to master our tongue.

Will Carleton says in his *First Settler's Story*—

"Boys flying kites haul in their white-winged birds;
You can't do that way when you're flying words.
Things that we think may sometimes fall back dead;
But God Himself can't kill them when they're said."

"Kind words never die." And every word fitly spoken is like an apple of gold in a basket of silver.

Second

"I shall be next unto thee."

1 SAM. xxiii. 17.

WHAT a kind, unselfish soul Jonathan was. His love and care for David we all admire. We have a sweet little picture of him here. David was keeping out of Saul's way because he was "seeking his life," and was getting evidently afraid and weary of being hunted. Jonathan met him in a wood (or perhaps a place called Horesh) privately, and tried to cheer him. He told him not to fear, "for the hand of Saul my father shall not find thee; and thou shalt be king over Israel. And I shall be next unto thee."

These were cheery, manly words, and there were, I doubt not, many more such. Jonathan meant what he said, and quite believed he would have the joy of seeing his friend on the throne. But before that time good, kind Jonathan was killed in battle, and we are not told that they ever met again after Horesh. If they had known it was their last meeting, Jonathan could not have said nobler words, or more surely have "strengthened David's hand in God."

Here was the king's son, next to the throne by

birth, doing all he could to encourage the shepherd's son to the highest place, while he is quite content to be second.

This is one of the things we all have to learn—namely, *how to take second place gracefully.*

There is a right ambition we all feel which makes us wish to be first. The school worker, if he is worth much, strives for the top place in class. The racer runs hard to come in first, and is glad when the winning cheer greets him. So it should be.

But we cannot always be first, and the great thing then is, like Jonathan, to see someone above us, before us, in the coveted place, without being angry or jealous or sulky. He is happy, indeed, who, without giving up true ambition, can say, " I shall be next," with all good feeling.

In the first place, I want you to remember that there are times when we *must* be next.

At home we have to take second place sometimes. The younger give place to the elders naturally. The visitor is always before those of the home. Our little guest must have first choice of everything, first turn at every game, first seat at table, first gift in presents; and we of the home should gladly be next.

There is the cleverer boy in our own class, who, do what we will, takes first place. Perhaps he does not work harder than you do, but you can't beat him.

Examination time comes, as come it will. You have been working very hard all the term to come out first. And when the list comes, you are down, and the one you feared is at the top. Now is the time to take second place cheerfully.

A girl the other day said to her successful rival, "I *hate* you for getting first." If she had possessed Jonathan's fine spirit, she would have said, "I tried hard to beat you, but you have fairly beaten me, and I congratulate you."

We cannot help people being older, and richer and cleverer and stronger than we are, so let us learn the simple gladness of being a good second.

Then let us remember, also, that there are times when we may *choose* to be second.

Jonathan was very likely the eldest of the king's sons, and had perhaps the natural claim to the throne. But because God has chosen David the peasant to be king, Jonathan gladly gives way, with a generous pride in his lowly friend's prospect, which is very praise-worthy.

So he takes second place, not because he must, but because he would.

Let me give you two further beautiful illustrations of this. Dr. Blow many years ago (he died 1708) was organist of Westminster Abbey. After holding this high position for eleven years, he gave it up of his own accord to one of his pupils, then only twenty-two years of age. He did this because he considered that he was more accomplished than himself, and therefore better able to serve the church as organist. This distinguished pupil worked for fifteen years, when he died, the Doctor all the while rejoicing greatly in his success. After his death, Dr. Blow again took his old place.

This was truly great: the position was his, but, for the sake of the cause he had at heart, he took second place. There are many causes and interests about us all that that are greater than we are, and for their sake *we* must sometimes consent to be second.

I read a noble story from Mr. Howatt, showing how a boy can be both high-minded and unselfish for the sake of another.

Jamie Pettigrew and Willie Hunter were the clever boys in Mr. Howatt's school class, and used "to run neck and neck for the prizes." Examination day came again. Jamie and Willie were left last in the field. Jamie missed question after question, which Willie answered, and he got the prize.

"I," says Mr. Howatt, "went home with Jamie that night, and instead of being cast down at losing the prize, he seemed rather to be mighty glad. I couldn't understand it.

"'Why, Jamie,' I said, 'you could have answered some of those questions; I know you could.'

"'Of course I could!' he said, with a laugh.

"'Then why didn't you?' I asked.

"He wouldn't answer for a while, but I kept pressing and pressing him, till at last he turned round, with such a strange, kind look in his bonnie brown eyes.

"'Look here,' he said; 'how could I help it? There's poor Willie—his mother died last week, and if it hadn't been Examination Day, he wouldn't have been at school. Do you think I was going to be so mean as to take a prize from a poor fellow who had just lost his mother?'"

Bravo, laddie! a good speech that; and second was a good place, if not the noblest of any in all the school that day.

Love for others, which Christ gives us, will often prompt us to be second, when we might, if we would, be first.

So you see in how many ways our text applies to us, and what a great lesson it teaches. Much of our joy, and the pleasure others will find in us depend upon our learning this lesson.

A boy said to me, "It's easy to be second—the difficulty is to get first." As he meant it, he was quite right. It is easier to go down than up. But it is not easy for one who wants to be first to take second place with good grace.

There are some boys who can't get out at cricket or go down in class, without bad temper—some girls who can't bear anyone else to be preferred or asked out to tea, without being jealous.

Remember Jonathan, boys and girls, and when you can't be first, or when love prompts you to give up first place, take second with good heart and true. Christ did it for us. "Though rich, He became poor, that through His poverty we might become rich."

A Riddle

"Out of the eater came forth meat, and out of the strong came forth sweetness." JUDGES xiv. 14.

A very interesting riddle comes to us from North Germany, which I fancy few of us could guess, try as we would.

The judges offered a woman her husband's life, if she could make a riddle which they could not guess. She made one as follows:—

> "As hitherwards on my way I sped,
> I took the living out of the dead.
> Six were thus of the seventh made quit:—
> To rede my riddle, my lords, 'tis fit."

They "gave it up," and the husband was spared. And what do you think the answer was? On her way to the court the woman found the carcase of a horse in which a bird had built its nest and hatched six young ones. These she took away, and thus "six were of the seventh made quit."

Just such a riddle was this of Samson's. He put it to the guests assembled at his wedding, and gave them seven days to guess it in. But they could not guess it. And I don't think they ever would, had they not got the answer from Samson's wife, who teased him until he told it her. Then, before the sun went down on the seventh day, they answered, "What is sweeter than honey? and what is stronger than a lion?"

A right answer, though they had got it in a mean way.

Where did Samson find his riddle first of all? He made it. And thus.

One day, going with his father and mother to Timnath visiting, he went ahead of his parents, being so much younger and faster than they. He rambled amongst the vines which grew on the hillsides, when suddenly a young lion sprang out and roared against him, desiring to have him. But there came upon Samson a spirit of courage and strength, so that he seized the lion and rent him like the cook rends the kid. He had no weapon, and thought so little of it that he did not tell his mother.

Then, about a year afterwards, going along the same road, he turned aside to see the dead lion, and there in the body, dried hard and made sweet by the sun, bees had deposited their honey, some of which he took and ate as he went.

Hence his riddle—"Out of the eater came forth meat, and out of the strong came forth sweetness." So his dead lion served him not only for a riddle, but gave him honey.

We may learn that *every victory we win will yield us some good*. Sin and temptation are the lions about our way which we must kill.

The errand boy going on his way sees boys playing marbles. He is tempted to put down his basket and to sit on the handle to watch the game. That is a loitering lion which he should kill, rather than kill his master's time and make people cross because the goods are not delivered.

At school one is tempted to love play-time so much that he hates work and won't do it. We should kill laziness, and we shall find that duty done is one of the sweetest pleasures. Idleness conquered will be like a dead lion with honey in it.

We are tempted to selfishness and greediness. This lion likes to keep all for himself, and he growls savagely if another comes near to his bone.

When I was at a little country school in Lincolnshire, we used to have hampers from home. Such hampers were they! Cakes, sweets, fruit, and all kinds of things dear to a schoolboy's heart. How eagerly we used to watch for the carrier's cart! But the rule was that we should share the contents with our schoolfellows, lest we should be greedy. And there was certainly as much pleasure in sharing as in eating.

The way to kill the greediness is to share what we have with others.

> "I have a plum cake, the whole is my own.
> And no one will know if I eat it alone—
> But what if the cake be so sweet and so nice?
> I daresay poor Jack would be glad of a slice.
> My treat he shall share, a *large* slice shall be his;
> For to eat all one's self—O how selfish it is!"

The prizes of conquest are many. Each victory over sin and temptation will make us stronger to conquer again.

Then we shall have also the joys of conquest. There is no gladness so great as that of doing right, and no pleasure so pure as that of conquering some untrue or unkind or selfish feeling in our hearts.

If you have made a good score at cricket, or done specially well in your music, you know the pleasure it brings. Thus "out of the strong will come forth sweetness."

Let us never forget that right has more pleasures than anything else in the world, that virtue has more honey than vice. "Wee Willie Winkie" tells this pretty story:—

The "blue-line" street-car stopped at the corner, and an anxious-looking young woman put a small boy inside.

"Now, Bob," she said, as she hurried out to the platform again, "don't lose that note I gave you; don't take it out of your pocket at all."

"No'm," said the little man, looking wistfully after his mother as the conductor pulled the strap, the driver unscrewed the brake, and the horses, shaking their bells, trotted off with the car.

"What's your name, Bob?" asked a mischievous-looking young man sitting beside him.

"Robert Cullen Deems," he answered.

"Where are you going?"

"To my grandma's."

"Let me see that note in your pocket."

The look of innocent surprise in the round face ought to have shamed the boy's tormentor, but he only said again, "Let me see it."

"I tan't," said Robert Cullen Deems.

"See here, if you don't, I'll scare the horses and make them run away."

The little boy cast an apprehensive look at the belled horses, and shook his head.

"Here, Bob, I'll give this peach if you'll pull that note half-way out of your pocket."

The boy did not reply, but some of the older people looked angry.

"I say, chum, I'll give you this whole bag of peaches if you will just show me the corner of your note," said the tempter.

The child turned away, as if he did not wish to hear any more, but the young man opened the bag and held it just where he could see and smell the luscious fruit.

A look of distress came into the boy's face; I believe Bob was afraid to trust himself, and when a man left his seat on the other end to get off the car, the little boy slid quickly down, left the temptation behind, and climbed into the vacant place.

A pair of prettily-gloved hands began almost unconsciously to clap, and then everybody clapped and applauded until it might have alarmed Bob, if a young lady sitting by had not slipped her arm around him and said—

"Tell your mamma that we all congratulate her upon having a little man strong enough to resist temptation and wise enough to run away from it."

I doubt if that long, hard message ever reached Bob's mother; but no matter, the note got to his grandmother without ever coming out of his pocket. And sturdy Bob had rich reward in doing right.

There is one other thing about Samson's success that I want you specially to remember—"the Spirit of the Lord came mightily upon him." Why was this? Because "he had nothing in his hand." He had no arrow, no club, no sword wherewith he could kill the lion. The Spirit of God made him strong enough to do it without weapon. *We* can't kill sin and temptation by ourselves; we must ask God to help us, and He always will.

When Samson was a small boy, it is said, "the child grew, and the Lord blessed him."

The Lord will bless us if we remember Him, and pray.

Clean Hands

"He that hath clean hands shall be stronger and stronger."
JOB xvii. 9.

ONE's hands will get dirty at play or at work. Children whose playground is the street come home with hands like sweeps, and no wonder! Boys who work in dirty trades get their hands dirty, and who could help it? But no one likes dirty hands if they are at all clean people. Father comes home from work, and one of the first things he does is to wash his hands. Mothers like clean hands, I know. When we come home from school, one of her first questions before we come to her snow-white table is, "Are your hands clean?" And before we can turn into our clean, white beds, the rule is that our hands shall be clean. And surely boys and girls won't get not to mind whether their hands are clean or dirty, though I have known some boys who didn't at all dislike dirty hands.

Fathers and mothers, boys and girls, like clean hands, and so does God. He speaks a good deal in His Word about them. One of the beautiful short psalms, speaking about those who shall stand in God's holy place, speaks of them first of all as having clean hands. God won't have in His holy place any dirty hands.

And the text before us speaks about the worth of clean hands — "He that hath clean hands shall be *stronger and stronger.*"

I need scarcely say that this does not mean clean hands in the ordinary sense; they may have some of the dirt of play and of honest work, and yet be clean hands in the meaning of the text.

1. In the Bible by clean hands is meant nearly always *honest* hands—hands that have not taken bribes, or what does not belong to them.

If anyone has done wrong, and he comes to you and says, "I will give you a penny not to tell," that is a bribe, and the hand that takes it is not clean.

Hands that never steal are so far clean. I was taught as a boy—

> " It is a sin to steal a pin,
> And so much more a greater thing."

To take a pin, a pear, a flower, a marble that is not ours is to have dirty hands.

They begin to get soiled by little things. A boy puts his hand through the railings to take flowers, and then, when he is older, into the master's till to take money.

But we must remember that God won't have dirty hands in His place, nor will they bring us any good.

2. *Kind* hands are clean hands. Fingers may be used to pinch your sister, or to untie the knots in her

string. Hands may be made into fists to fight with, or spread out for the help of others: like the boy who guided across the busy street the woman

> "Who was old, and feeble, and grey,
> And bent with the chill of the winter's day."

Our hands are more liable to become dirty in reference to the dumb creatures about us than in any other way.

The hand that pushes the cat into the stream, or throws the stone at the street dog, the fingers that pull legs from flies, and stick pins into cockchafers, are not clean. God cares for these things very much, and looks that our hands shall be clean in kindness to them.

3. *Busy* hands are clean. We all remember the old saying—

> "Satan finds some mischief still
> For idle hands to do."

The Italians have a proverb which says, "He that labours is tempted by one devil; he that is idle by a thousand." There is much truth in this. The hands that are most likely to be kept clean are those busily engaged upon some useful work. Our fingers are useful instruments of the will, and by the help of tools, such as the needle and the saw, can make wonderful things. Let your hands be busy. Sew the garment, weed the garden, make the mouse-cage. Let them carry flowers to the sick, or help the tired child in the street with her big bundle.

4. *Consecrated* hands are clean. When Paul speaks about men praying, he says, "I desire that the men pray in every place, lifting up *holy hands.*"

The hands come into our prayer specially. The Jews and early Christians raised their palms towards heaven, indicating the offering of their petition and their readiness to receive what God had to give. We fold our hands in token of our submission to God. I think at first the uplifting of the hands—"the instruments of our necessities"—was a giving of them to God. They were held up in token that they were His. Thus the hands that had been kept free from violence and impurity were "holy," and were lifted up to God.

Let our prayer be—

> "Take my hands, and let them move
> At the impulse of Thy love."

There is no surer way of keeping them clean.

And our text speaks also of the value of clean hands. He who has them shall be stronger and stronger. Knowing his hands are clean, he will have that clear conscience which makes men so strong and joyous.

Boys with clean hands won't have to skulk and put them in their pockets lest anyone sees them. They don't fear about being found out. How pleased we are to hold out hands when asked if they are clean when we know that they are! A good conscience, boys and girls, is a tower of strength to us.

Let us all see to it that our hands are clean, for

God won't have dirty ones. I remember in a public library where they lent books to be read in the room, there was a notice on the walls that the hands must be clean. If anyone went for a book who had not kept the rule, the attendant would refuse the book until the hands were washed. I saw once quite a big fellow sent off to wash his hands.

In God's holy place all hands must be clean.

But supposing we have got them dirty, what shall we do? Can we wash our hands if unkindness, dishonesty, or impurity has soiled them? Yes, we must ask God to forgive, to help us to do better, and then keep them clean by taking care.

"I will wash my hands in innocency,
So will I compass Thine altar, O Lord."

Play-dirt, work-dirt, easily comes off, and though sin-dirt is more difficult to remove, yet it can be washed away.

A Pure Heart

"He that hath clean hands and a pure heart."
Ps. xxiv. 4.

In our last sermon we were speaking about clean hands. Now I want you to think about pure hearts.

The hymn in which the text is found is a very beautiful one. The ark of Jehovah, which has been for about three months in the house of Obed-Edom, is being taken to Jerusalem in great pomp. The wonderful procession of king and priests and people wound up the mountain-side to the city. As they went they sang this 24th Psalm as a kind of choral hymn. All the people sang together the first and second verses, and then one choir sang this question—

"Who shall ascend the hill of the Lord?
Who shall stand in His holy place."

And another choir answered—

"He that is of clean hands, and pure of heart."

Then, as they neared the "old grey fortress," they all sent up a mighty sound of song—

"Lift up your heads, O ye gates!"

Then priests and Levites within the city asked in song—

"Who is this King of glory?"

And the people burst out again in triumphant strains—

"The Lord strong and mighty,
The Lord mighty in battle."

So they joyously bear the ark to the holy place, where all who stand must have clean hands and pure hearts. We said before that clean hands are honest, kind, busy, and holy hands. Let us now see what pure hearts are.

1. They are *loving* hearts.

They love good desires, good deeds, good people, and, above all, they love God.

When we have pure hearts, we love to pray. We do not simply say our prayers because we have to do so, but because we like to do so. We love play, it is true, and ought to as long as we are young, but we must not love playing instead of praying.

Bad people don't love people because they are good. "Birds of a feather flock together," says the old proverb. You can generally tell the character of a girl or boy by the company they keep. Pure-hearted boys won't like the company of those who use bad words and do base things.

God, too, we love, when our hearts are clean. His will and His ways we approve.

2. They are *hating* hearts also.

When a girl was asked if she had a new heart, her reply was, "Yes, I hope so, because I love the things which I used to hate, and hate what I used to love."

Yes, quite so. Badness is hateful to us when our hearts are right. Sin is ugly, and only ugly, when we have really learned to love good. If ever we are beginning to think lightly of sin, to feel that it is rather jolly, to prefer coarse words to gentle ones, lies to truth, it is because our hearts are not pure.

3. Pure hearts are *new* hearts.

We have none of us in ourselves all we need to make our hearts pure. We all have our good points, traits of character that commend us to others. But we have also traits of evil. Hence we must have new hearts given to us by God. That is, we need God's Spirit to create in us new loves, and renew our will to do right, and to cleanse our hearts from evil.

Hence the prayer we all know so well—"Create in me a clean heart, O God," and the great promise—"A new heart also will I give you."

The Rev. E. Payson Hammond, a great child-lover, tells this story. One day a boy, scarcely four years old, came running to his mother and said, "Mamma, I said a naughty word; I sweared, I did."

"Did you?" she said. "Come here, then, and I will get some clean water and a rag and some soap, and wash your mouth out."

She then carefully went to work, and washed his mouth out thoroughly, and when she pressed her finger down into his throat in a half-choking way, he said—

"What are you doing that for?"

"Because I want to get down into your heart, and wash your heart out, but I see that I can't do that, so you will have to ask God to do that for you."

"How can God do it?"

"I do not know. He does not tell me."

"I know it came from the heart, because I thought the naughty word before I said it. But will He do it if I ask Him."

"Yes, He will. He promises to do so."

"Then I will ask Him."

Away he went to his room, and, kneeling down, he said—

"O God, I said a naughty word. I sweared, I did. Mamma has washed my mouth out, but she can't wash my heart out. O God, please wash my heart out. For Jesus' sake. Amen."

If some of the words in this prayer seem strange, you must remember that he was only a very little fellow. Years afterwards, the mother said that her boy was changed from that day. God gave him a new heart that kept him from bad words.

God will do the same for us, if we ask. We can't make them pure ourselves. If my watch goes wrong, I don't try to repair it myself. It is so delicate and intricate that I should spoil it, so I take it to the watchmaker.

Why do you think clean hands and pure hearts are thus joined together in the text? Because they have much to do with one another in the life. The surest way to secure clean hands is to have a pure heart. If my hands are cruel, it is because my heart is cruel. As the wee boy said, "I *thought* the naughty word before I said it."

The hands of the clock do not go by themselves. If they are out of time, or stop, no one thinks of blaming them. We know there must be something wrong with the works. Spring and wheels within make them go, or cause them to stop.

So with our life : the heart regulates the hands.

Here the pure heart is our greatest need for every day, and for God's holy place. Through the old gates of Jerusalem some, I daresay, went into the holy place who were not either clean of hand or pure of heart, but nothing unclean can enter the holier city.

"There shall in no wise enter into it anything unclean."

We shall not get to heaven, if our hearts are not new.

God's best gift is the pure heart, and if we go to God, He will keep His promise, and give us it.

A rabbi asked his pupils this question—"What is the best thing for a man to possess?" I wonder what answer we should give? Well, listen to theirs. One said, "A kind nature"; another, "A good companion"; another, "A good neighbour"; but another, named Eleazer, said, "A good heart."

"I like your answer best, Eleazer," said the dear master, "*for it includes all the rest.*"

Copper Precious as Gold

"Two vessels of fine bright brass, precious as gold."
Ezra viii. 27 (R.V.).

These were amongst the vessels of God's house which Ezra restored. There were there costly bowls of gold and beautiful vessels of silver, and amongst them two vessels of fine copper, or, as the Revised Version reads, "fine bright brass," precious as gold.

Any boy or girl, if asked whether gold or copper was the more valuable, would answer "Gold," and if offered a new penny or an old sovereign, would choose the latter. And so the bowl of gold, however small, would be worth more than the vessel of brass, however great in the common sense of worth. But the word "precious" refers not so much to the metal the vessels were made of as to the usefulness of the vessels themselves. We might say "two vessels of fine copper, desirable as gold."

For the work of God's house they were as necessary as the silver and gold vessels. There may also be a reference to their form; so exquisite were they in workmanship that the only way to speak of them was "precious as gold."

Now these vessels of common metal amongst those

of more precious metal stand to me for the everyday, trifling things of life well done.

Miss Yonge has written a book called *A Book of Golden Deeds*. In it she tells of the wonderful and heroic but rare things which people have done, and are worth remembering. Here is one of a French officer in the Seven Years' War. France had taken the side of Austria, you remember, against Germany. Louis XV. had sent a French army into Germany. This officer was sent out alone into a wood to reconnoitre. Suddenly he found himself surrounded by a number of soldiers whose bayonets pricked his breast, and a voice whispered in his ear, " Make the slightest noise, and you are a dead man." In a moment he understood it. The enemy were advancing to surprise the French, and would be upon them when night was further advanced. He did not hesitate a moment, but shouted his loudest, " Here, Auvergne! Here are the enemy!"

By the time his cry reached the ears of his men, he was dead, but his death saved the army. That is worth telling and recording among the "Golden Deeds." I doubt not that we should all like to be on that roll of illustrious ones for some great deed nobly done.

But there is another book, not yet written, in which we may all be enrolled. I should call it " A Book of Common Deeds well done." We don't keep such a book, but God does.

Let me illustrate what I mean.

If your brother fell into the river, and you jumped in

and rescued him, that would be like a golden deed which your schoolfellows would talk about, and for which they would, perhaps, give you an innings at cricket.

But to play with your little brother when he wants a game and you don't; to be kind to him when he is cross; to cheer his tears away when he is in sorrow, is like doing copper deeds. No one save our mother talks about them, but before her and God they are precious as gold.

The noblest everywhere are those who are not above doing the least things.

He who shines in the field, but is mean in the home, is a despicable character.

He who turns up when there is anything big to do, but "can't bother" when it is something commonplace that won't bring him any special pleasure or credit, is a very little-souled creature.

Don't forget the vessels of *copper*.

Let us remember also the form of the copper. It was "fine," or, taking the verse as read, "fine bright brass." What is that? Polished, made to shine, like the copper kettles in Yorkshire cottages. They were not made of dim, unprepared metal. This speaks to us about *the way in which we are to do our common deeds*.

They are to be polished. There are three ways particularly in which we can make the smallest deed shine like "fine bright brass."

1. By *gentleness*.

Rudeness, roughness will spoil any deed. As three

boys went home from school in the snow, they saw an old organ-grinder who wore a top hat. What a target! One, two, three snowballs, and the hat rolled into the snow. Did the old grinder swear and turn cross? No, he smiled and said, "Now I'll play you a tune to make you merry."

A small thing, but splendidly done.

2. By *cheerfulness*.

To do a thing as if you were obliged to, and were cross about it, is to have the metal very unpolished. And to do a disagreeable thing grumpily is to make it more and more disagreeable.

You come home from school, and are about to go out for a game when mother calls, wanting you for an errand or some little reasonable service. If you reply, "Yes, mother," as if you were very much disappointed and very cross, the copper is not at all polished; but if you reply, "Yes, mother," in a cheery tone which says, "I will do anything for you," that is like "fine bright brass."

Yes, cheerfulness makes the hardest duty easier and the smallest service fine.

3. *Unselfishness* is also a wonderful polisher.

When we are bestowing our little gifts upon others, our giving is often like unpolished copper. When, for instance, you give what you have grown tired of or don't like or don't want, that is better than not giving at all, but it is not the best gift. When we give what we should very much like to keep, then our gift is like the "fine copper."

Two farthings, when they are all ourstore and given in a true spirit, may be—Christ said once they were—"precious as gold," while two sovereigns may not be worth a flint stone when given in another way.

It was breaking-up day, and the school sports were fixed for two o'clock. Richie left home in good time to start in the first race for a pair of running-shoes and a cricket-cap. On his way he found a letter by the roadside. On the envelope above the address was IMMEDIATE. Someone had evidently intended to put it in the pillar-box for twelve o'clock clearance. The General Post-Office, where it must go if it was to be delivered that day, was a long way off, and he would have to run hard to get there and back in time for his race, and then, tired with the run, he might lose it. Richie hesitated, and then, thinking the letter might be very important to someone, away he ran. In the race he made a good start, but Willie Webb beat him at the finish. Richie was sorely disappointed, and went home not sure whether the letter was worth this loss. During the night Mrs. Webb's stacks were on fire, and Richie with his father went to help put it out. In her fear and trouble Mrs. Webb said, "I renewed the insurance only to-day." Then Willie said to Richie, "Whatever shall I do? I lost the letter." Richie asked what it was like, and then said, "Don't worry, old fellow. I found it, and posted it for you." And thus Mrs. Webb got her insurance, and she gave Richie the best cricket-cap and running-shoes that could be bought. So his little unselfish deed was like the vessel of " fine copper, precious as gold."

If then we cannot do wonderful things, let us do the common things wonderfully. Gideon was busy " beating out wheat in the winepress " when God's call to the highest service for his country came to him. The commonplace duty led to the greatest honour. Never slight the little things.

Dr. Richard Newton tells us that the most beautiful stained glass window in Lincoln Cathedral was made by an apprentice out of little pieces of glass that had been thrown aside by his master as useless. The lines that someone has written about this window are worth remembering in connection with our subject of the copper deeds.

> " Great things are made of fragments small,
>   Small things are germs of great;
> And, of earth's stately temples, all
>   To fragments owe their weight.
>
> This window, peer of all the rest,
>   Of fragments small is wrought;
> Of fragments that the artist deemed
>   Unworthy of his thought.
>
> And thus may we, of little things,
>   Kind words and gentle deeds,
> Add wealth or beauty to our lives
>   Which greater acts exceeds.
>
> Each victory o'er a sinful thought,
>   Each action true and pure,
> Is, 'mid our life's engraving, wrought
>   In tints that shall endure."

Straight Away

"And straightway they left the nets and followed Him."
MARK i. 18.

Two brothers, fishermen, were busy at their work, just as busy and earnest as fishermen could be. They were both casting a net and drawing in their fish. Then along the shore, where the tiny waves washed up the shingle, Jesus was seen walking. He said to the brothers, "Come after Me, and I will make you to become fishers of men." And directly they left boat and nets, work and fish, and followed Him.

I daresay there are some boys and girls who wonder at this, and think if they had a boat and nets they wouldn't leave them and follow Christ. Yes, it does seem strange at first, but let us think about it and see what there is in it. We will consider first what they did, then why they did it, and then how they did it.

1. *What they did.*

"They *left the nets.*"

This means very much to these fishers. The nets were their means of livelihood. But that word is too long—they got their bread by fishing with their nets, and in leaving them they were leaving their business.

The nets were the most they could leave, and they did not hesitate to leave them.

Before we boys and girls can become Christians—if we are not such already—there is something we have to leave. When the voice of Christ comes to us, it says, "*leave* all and *follow* Me." We have not to give up home or school or business, pleasure or play, but everything that keeps us from being Christians.

We must leave bad habits and bad companions, naughty words and naughty deeds. All sin we have to leave to follow Christ. To begin to love Christ we must begin to give up sin.

Then in Christ's *service* we often have to leave much else. Many have given up home and pleasure to do good to others for Christ's sake. That call may come to some of you some day.

Like these brother fishers, whatever Christ bids us leave, let us do it.

2. *Why they did it.*

"And *followed Him.*" These words carry the secret of their great giving up. Think again how much they left, and then remember that they did it for sake of "following Him."

Christ and His service were worth more to them than boats and nets. They would have the friendship of Christ Himself. And that would be worth a good many nets. Jesus seemed worth more to these fishers than anything else in the world. And so they quickly left what they were doing and followed Him.

Now, boys and girls, this is just true for all of us. Christ is better than anything else life has. Nothing brings so much joy and pleasure and good into our life as Christ.

Then they would have also Christ's service: "I will make you to become fishers of men." Christ was going to make them of use to other men. And that was better than the best fishing.

I think, boys and girls, that the greatest joy in being Christ's lovers is that we can help others to be good.

You all know how very, very often bad boys and girls make others bad. Ministers and teachers warn us against evil companions, because they will make us evil. It is just as true that good people make others good. Goodness is far stronger and more attractive than badness. When we belong to Christ, He uses our life to help others and to save them.

Thus, when these brothers thought of their boats and nets and fishing, and of Christ and His service, they left all and followed Him.

If I offered to give a sovereign for each penny you have, would you be long in deciding to give up the penny? If anyone would make such an offer to me, I should quickly hunt up all my pennies and get them changed.

It is much like that when we leave anything for Christ. We are exchanging our pence for sovereigns. We may give up much, but we shall always get more.

3. *How they did it.*

"And *straightway*." This is a good word and worth remembering. It means immediately, "on the spot," as we say sometimes; or *straight away*. They did not hesitate or loiter or wonder, but followed straight away.

It is always best to do the right at once. The nasty little spoilers of life are well known to us. "Wait a minute," says the boy when his mother calls. "I am going to," says another, who knows he ought to have done something long ago. "I will by and by," says a third, who is excusing neglect of present duty. These are like little foxes that spoil the grapes. We shall never do anything much in life if we let them into our vineyard.

No, the splendid word is *straight away* for everything. The great successes of life are won by men and women who don't wait, but do the duty of the moment at once.

It is said that Dr. Adam Clarke, who was himself a scholar, had a neighbour, a scholar also. They both learned overnight that the bookseller had a rare Greek Testament for sale, and they both (unknown to one another) made up their minds to purchase it if possible. The neighbour hastened over his breakfast, and went to the shop, sure that he must be the first customer of the day, and asked to see the rare book. "You are too late," said the bookseller. "Impossible!" said the scholar. "I have only just had my breakfast, and have come straight away." "Yes," said the bookseller; "but Dr. Clarke came *before breakfast.*"

"Before breakfast" got the coveted book. "STRAIGHT-WAY they left the nets and followed Him."

It is not so true of anything else as of following Christ—that the best way to do it is straight away.

Dogs

"Beware of the dogs."
PHIL. iii. 2 (R.V.).

WE should scarcely expect to find such a text, but here it is. And what can it mean? Well, let us see.

Dogs in St. Paul's day were not exactly like our dogs. He did not feel about them as we do. We keep them in the house, and feed them, and nurse and pet them. But when Paul wrote, they were a bit of a nuisance and a danger also. Big, masterless, savage dogs prowled about the villages and cities, seeking their food. They would snap, and snarl, and bite, so that you needed a strong stick, and to be on your guard.

And so, when St. Paul wanted to warn his friends against people who were unkind, cruel, and hurtful, he thought about these stray dogs, and said, "Beware of the dogs."

And the text has a voice for us to-day, for just as these dogs ran about the streets hither and thither, looking this way and that, ever ready to snap and bite, so there are people about school and playground, street and workplace, who are like them, and the text would say, Beware of the boys and girls who will bite you.

1. *Dogs to mind.*

(*a*) Sly dogs.—Boys, for instance, who will tempt you to loiter on your way to school or as you are going an errand. They say it doesn't matter if you are a little late.

Beware of those tempting boys and girls who entice us to do wrong, promising us all sorts of nice things if only we won't be so particular. They tempt us often to break the rule of home which says we are not to go to certain places and we are to be in at certain times. "What does it matter? Mothers don't know everything," says our sly, tempting dog. I never knew a mother who said or thought she did know everything, but I am quite sure she knows more than we do, and that her law is very good.

So whenever anyone is tempting you not to care then remember this text, "Beware of the dogs."

(*b*) Savage dogs.—There are some boys and girls who are like *savage* dogs. They use bad words, they do nasty and dirty things. Beware of them, for they will injure you, and will never be content until you do as they do. Of all evil things, evil companions are the most evil.

Beware of anybody and everybody round about you who would try to do you harm. There are many sorts, rough and smooth, sly and savage. But the most dangerous of all is the sly dog. He wags his tail as if pleased to see you, and when you go to stroke him, he snaps at you.

2. Why "beware of the dogs"? Because they bite and bring us no good.

A father brought his boy six red, round, ripe apples, just such as the boy loved. He looked at them with boyish delight. "Six" said he; "thank you very much!" Then he was going to stow them away where we put all our treasures of the moment—string, top, knife, marbles, nails, and coppers, with a few sweets on occasion.

"No, no," said the father; "you must not put them in your pocket." "Then I'll eat them." "No; put them in the cupboard." "In the cupboard?" exclaimed the disappointed laddie. There he had to place them. A nice little group they were. Then the father gave him another, and said, "Put this one with them." "But it's rotten, and will spoil the others." But he had to do it. A nasty one amongst six rosy, ripe ones. And there they stayed until he was told he might have them. Then he found the nasty one had made them all nasty. "There," he said; "I knew it would be so." "And so did I," said the father. "And my boy will find, if he will play with bad boys who swear and steal, they will spoil him too."

You see what the father meant by his lesson. If you don't want your apples spoiled, keep them away from the bad one. And if you don't want yourself spoiled, keep away from bad boys and girls.

A man had a board by his dog-kennel with the words "Beware of the dog" painted in very large letters. A friend said to him, "I suppose you have had that written in such big letters, that he who runs may read, have you?" "No," he said, "I have not. I have put it in good big letters, that he who reads may run."

Boys and girls, if ever you find anyone try to make you say a bad word or do a mean, bad thing, then have this text before you in big, big letters—

"Beware of the Dogs."

Remember

"Remember Jesus Christ."
2 Tim. ii. 8 (R.V.).

We should never forget our best friends, though we do so sometimes. The boy who thinks of his schoolfellow who gave him his first knife forgets the friend who bound up his cut finger. We think more of those who please us than those who help us. Hence, people who give us things are remembered after those who have taught us are forgotten. Those who bring us presents occasionally are thought of, while those who are always giving to us what we most need are unremembered. Thus is it that auntie often gets thanks, while mother gets none.

We must not forget our best friends, and certainly we must never forget Him who is more than friend.

Paul tells Timothy to "remember Jesus Christ," and I am sure he would say so to every boy and girl to-day.

Here, then, is a PLEASANT DUTY—"Remember Christ."

That is, *think about* Him. You boys and girls who read have come across many men and women who have impressed your mind, and you think of them long after the reading. Who does not remember St. George, who slew the dragon? Or Robinson Crusoe, who cared for "Friday"? So also we think about the great characters of history, King Alfred, Nelson, Gordon, and many others. Let us think about the greatest of them all, Jesus Christ. Never was one like Him. What wonderful things He did! What wise and kind words He spoke! The verse tells Timothy what particularly he was to think about. "Jesus Christ *risen from the dead.*"

The people killed Him on the cruel cross. Kind hands buried Him in the new grave, before which the soldiers rolled a big stone, so that no one should steal the body. But in the morning the grave was empty. Jesus had risen, and He saw and talked with His disciples many times. Thus they knew that He was the Son of God, and not a deceiver, as the people said; their Saviour, and not a mere man like one of themselves. "Remember also," says Paul, "Jesus Christ of the seed of David." He was the one whom God had promised to give to them. And He shared their nature as well as being God. He was King of heaven, but also babe of Bethlehem. He could work miracles, making blind people see and dead people live; but He had been a boy, with play and lessons like other boys. Though God, He came and shared our lot. "Though rich, for our sakes He became poor, that we . . . might become rich."

Let us read and think about Him. But to remember Christ is TO LOVE Him and BE TRUE to Him.

The remembrance Christ Himself loves most of all is

our love. The boy remembers his mother most who loves her best. And he loves her best who is careful to do her will, who does what she would like, and avoids what she would disapprove.

When John Paton, who became the great missionary, left his home to go to Glasgow, forty miles had to be done on foot. His father walked with him the first six miles, and then they parted. The father and son were very dear to one another, and the parting was a sorrowful one. "God bless you, my son; your father's God prosper you and keep you from all evil," said the father.

After going some distance, John climbed the dyke to see if his father was standing where he left him. At the same moment the father climbed the dyke to see his son. John saw him get down. "I watched," he says, "through blinding tears till his form faded from my gaze; and then, hastening on my way, *vowed deeply and oft, by the help of God, to live and act so as never to grieve or dishonour such a father and mother as He had given me.*" That was the right way to remember his father and mother.

So, boys and girls, should we remember Christ. Act so as never to grieve Him or dishonour His name.

Paul tells Timothy to remember Christ, not simply because gratitude for what Christ had done for him should make him remember. He was speaking to him about "suffering hardship, as a good soldier of Jesus Christ"; so that he might be a good soldier he would have him remember Christ.

When we are tempted to do wrong, when we are in sorrow, when duty is difficult, when joys are many, remember Jesus Christ. Remember that He is near, that He is our Saviour, and that He will help us.

Whoever else you forget, don't forget Christ. We have never seen Him, but He sees us. We do not hear Him coming, but He is always with us. His gifts are bestowed every day, but they are the most precious of all we have. If Christ did not remember us, we should not have much to make our lives happy.

A mother was talking to her little girl about loving God. The child replied, "Mother, I have never seen God, how can I love Him?" A few days afterwards she received a lovely book from a friend. What pictures there were in that book! The more she turned over the leaves, the happier the wee maid felt, until at last she exclaimed, "Oh, mother, how I do love the good lady that sent me this book!"

"But you never saw her, my dear," said her mother.

"No," answered the child; "but I love her because she has sent me this present." So the child loved and remembered the lady whom she had never seen because of what she had sent her. Christ gave Himself for us. All the blessings of life come to us through Him, and in the future life He will give us much more.

Boys and girls, "Remember Jesus Christ."

THE END.

www.ingramcontent.com/pod-product-compliance
Lightning Source LLC
Chambersburg PA
CBHW030308170426
43202CB00009B/913